THE LETTERS OF P.O.G

*The Collective Mental Meanderings
of an Octogenarian Grandad*

THE LETTERS OF P.O.G

The Collective Mental Meanderings
of an Octogenarian Grandad

James F. Squire P.O.G.

The Book Guild Ltd
Sussex, England

The Book Guild Ltd.
25 High Street,
Lewes, Sussex

First published 1996
© James F. Squire 1996
Set in Palatino
Typesetting by Southern Reproductions (Sussex)
Crowborough, Sussex
Printed in Great Britain by
Bookcraft (Bath) Ltd.

A catalogue record for this book is
available from the British Library

ISBN 1 85776 075 1

CONTENTS

Family Tree

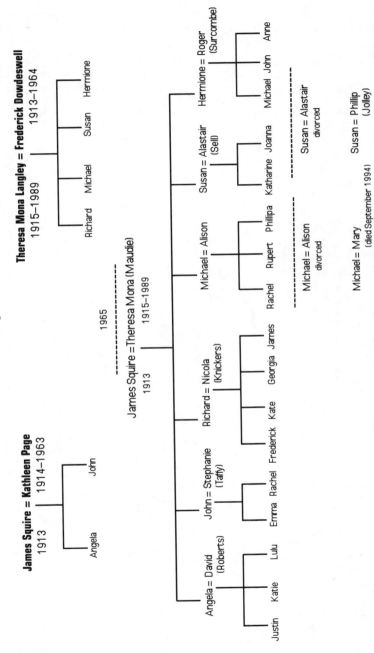

INTRODUCTION

James Squire, (alias P.O.G.), was born in Guildford, Surrey in 1913. He was a mistake. His parents already had a very voracious brood and could ill-afford an addition. However, James survived and was educated at the Royal Grammar School although one report was said to read, 'A model student but not a working model'.

On leaving school, he actually matriculated. It was decided that he would study architecture and was articled to a local firm. It was not a success. James rebelled and went to work on a national poultry farm. The attentions of an obnoxious female brought his labours to an end and from there he enjoyed a spell working for F W Woolworth in their nothing-over-sixpence store. But it was not to last and in a fit of desperation he enlisted as a trooper in the most famous of His Majesty's cavalry regiments. His love of horses and the comradeship that he found resulted in thirty-two years of service under four monarchs: King George V, Edward VIII, George VI and our present Queen, who was also his Colonel-in-Chief of the 16th/5th Lancers. He was commissioned with the rank of Captain.

He married a beautiful girl, had two children and spent twenty-five years carrying them around the world with him. It was his children that affectionately referred to their parents as P.O.D. and P.O.M. (Poor Old Dad and Poor Old Mum).

Tragedy struck them when P.O.M. was killed while he was serving in Germany.

Some years later he remarried – the widow of his best friend, a friendship that dated back to the Royal Grammar School. He also inherited a further four stepchildren with ages ranging from ten years to twenty. The two families integrated happily and all the children subsequently married and produced between them seventeen grandchildren.

And so P.O.D. became P.O.G.

A further happy twenty-five years passed until his second wife became ill and died from a malignant cancer after bravely suffering three pain-filled years.

Now approaching the age of the octogenarian P.O.G. bought himself a word processor and spent a year writing the story of his adventurous life. It is still on the shelf.

It was then that he started writing the letters of P.O.G. to the six families now spread over the world. It was a family tie keeping everyone in touch with one another. Then friends and other relations began to request copies so that P.O.G.'s mailing list became a financial burden.

P.O.G. continues writing. It keeps, to quote Monsieur Poirot, the grey matter working even if the outer shell is becoming increasingly fragile.

I hope that the letters of P.O.G. will afford the reader some amusement and pleasure.

THE LETTERS OF P.O.G
1992

Dear All,

Having completed the story of my life up to Mr William Shakespeare's sixth age I feel that I should now start on age number seven.

In second childishness and mere oblivion,
Sans teeth, sans eyes, sans taste, sans everything.

In just a few weeks I shall be embarking into the year of the octogenarian. What a stupid word. On par with dinosaur.

Extinct. Perhaps I too am extinct. I must admit that I am more and more confused by the affairs of this brave new world of mayhem and demonstrations. I am becoming lost in the babble of voices raised in protest about every conceivable subject under the sun. Even the sun and the greenhouse effect are major issues.

Poor old Grandad. It's all my fault.

Sans teeth. At least with my false choppers a plate of porridge presents no problems although barbecued chicken or sooty chops are beyond my powers of masticastion.

Sans eyes. This is overcome by three pairs of spectacles and a monocle. One pair of specs for reading, one for watching the television and one pair for driving. The driving ones enable me to see other motorists at twenty-five yards. I only see the back as they pass since they put the speed limit up to 90 mph. At least that seems to be the speed they are going as they passs me.

Reading a number plate at twenty-five yards is impossible, although I can generally get an impression of the colour as they flash by. The monocle is a standby if either of the other visual aids get lost.

Sans taste. Nothing seems to taste as it used to. Beer is a chemical mess and a gin and tonic or a Martini are ruined by the exorbitant cost. You will hear more on that subject in a later letter when I get on to finance.

Sans everything. At least modern medicine had provided me with replacement hips so that I am mobile without pain.

My ears are electric with facilities for increasing or decreasing the volume of sound at my own convenience. I can even switch off when conversation becomes a bore.

So, on the verge of extinction, one of the last Englishman before we all become European, I am also semi-bionic. Since Granny Maudie left me alone in this world of strife I have learnt to survive. I even use the washing machine with its eighteen programmes. (I only use programme no. 3) I cook and keep the old homestead reasonably clean and tidy. I have progressed as far as recording programmes by video although I have not the foggiest idea of how it works.

And I am not alone. This desirable dwelling situated in this much sought-after village is also the home of Samson. I do not have a cat. The cat has a human. Samson was the last anniversary gift that I gave to Granny Maudie. She asked for a black cat and it had to be male. She could not longer ride her broomstick but she intended to leave me with an educated feline. Samson welcomes me with open claws whenever I come in. After searching every cattery in Hampshire and Surrey I eventually bailed him out from a cat's prison near Frensham. It cost me the earth to bail him out, and then only with a written agreement that I paid for his membership to the Cats Protection League. He is a fully paid up member. Even as a kitten I soon realised that Sam was no ordinary household pet. He never to the best of my knowledge had the opportunity of riding a besom but Maudie taught him all she knew.

Sam had two main dislikes. Firstly people. He does not like being fondled although he does when he feels so inclined jump into my lap to have his head scratched. His second hate is television which proves how intelligent he is. He just leaves the room if it is switched on. Snooker, with no sound, he might watch for a short while.

'Cats would buy Whiskers' is erroneous in Sam's book. He will eat it and any other tinned cat food as a last resort but his favourite diet is a fat freshly caught mouse washed down with the cream from the top of the milk.

So Sam and I live in pleasant harmony. He is a man's cat and I am a cat's man.

Now I must stop. Perhaps my next letter will be more interesting.

As always,

Your P.O.G.

*   *   *

29 May 1992

Dear All,

Being old has its compensations. One can voice outrageous statements and no one takes the slightest bit of notice. The same applies when one sometimes talks sense.

I thought that I was dreaming when I saw and heard on the six o'clock news the Bailiff of Jersey and his followers demanding freedom from the yoke of oppression imposed on them by the British.

Your own P.O.G.

*   *   *

30 May 1992

Dear Hermione,

Jersey under the jackboot. British this time, not German.

What a load of codswallop!

Let me tell you about Jersey. Many years ago when I retired and joined the ranks of the OAPs your mother expressed a desire to return to the land of her youth, Jersey.

She was educated at the Jersey Ladies' College although she always said that she must have been the last lady because after she graduated they changed the name to Jersey Girls' College.

I suggested that she flew over to do a reconnaissance.

She did. Two days later she rang me up.

'We might as well pitch a tent in Piccadilly as come here,' she stated. 'The place is knee deep in motor cars.'

An understatement. It was up to the neck. Jersey was out. She

5

found Alderney which she assured me was unspoilt and was what Jersey was like when she was young.

Where shall I start? Jersey potatoes. Now grubby, dirty little objects on sale in the supermarket.

Jersey Royals, £1.69 a pound. Will they drop the Royal?

Maudie assured me that Jersey Royals were the best potatoes in the world. They may have been once. She said that they got their flavour from the seaweed that the farmers gathered from the beaches to fertilise the land. Either the seaweed has become polluted or they are using a different fertiliser because they certainly don't taste the same today. Maybe it's my palate.

Motor cars. As mentioned before, neck deep. It is virtually impossible to park a car anywhere. One just drives around till out of petrol. Thousands of them with 'H' plates on. The inhabitants mostly drive Porches, Ferraris, Mercedes or Rolls. As the island has a 30 mph speed limit they can hardly ever get out of first gear. It always amazed me how Jim Bergerac managed to slip easily into a parking spot and that there were never any other cars except police cars or Charlie's Rolls. There is a permanent haze of carbon monoxide over St Hellier. It puts Hong Kong in second place.

On the glorious beaches in the height of summer one can breathe in the perfume of suntan lotion and aftershave. An occasional waft of sea-salt breeze can be noticed if the breeze is off the sea.

One can sometimes, if one can afford it, indulge in a lobster lunch and years ago an ormer could be found. Skin-diving has virtually made them extinct now.

There are of course duty-free drinks and cigarettes. An alcoholic haze does help to deaden the pain. Maudie termed it Jersey Sunstroke.

'NO VAT' signs in the shops. It seemed to me that I could buy the same article at home for the same price including the VAT.

Jersey cream. Jersey butter. Jim Bergerac could probably locate a Jersey cow for you. Where they keep them is a mystery. The only Jersey herds that I know are in England. There is one large one that I know of in Shropshire, a little place called

Lydbury North on the Plowden Estate It seems that there are a few connoisseurs that keep them, rather in the same way that vintage cars are kept. I expect they export their butter and cream to Jersey.

One can of course always visit the Butterfly Farm, or the Strawberry Farm and there is a super leisure centre almost as good as Alton Towers. Again there are the remains of the awful German Occupation. I could go on but I think I have illustrated my point.

Now they are reeling under the British jackboot. Poor Jersey.

However, worry not. I for one do not intend to goosestep in my jackboots through St Hellier.

Hail Britannia!

Mr John Bull
(Alias P.O.G.)

* * *

1 June 1992

Dear All,

I am not at all sure that I like being in this seventh age. It's rather like being in limbo. A region of forgotten things, neglect, oblivion.

I get up each morning without any great enthusiasm. I force myself to make an effort. A cup of tea while I watch the BBC Morning News. I finish my tea more depressed than ever. Even the weather forecast is discouraging but as it is seldom correct I ignore it.

To the bathroom. The reflection in my mirror as I shave is even more discouraging than the weather. The ravages of time have taken their toll. The excesses of a mispent youth are plainly visible. A layer of white soapy lather improves it. Lack of concentration and a shaking hand nicks a portion of flesh from just below my left ear. At least I bleed well. It takes half a roll of toilet paper before the wound is under control. The towel is a bloody mess and as I put it into the soiled linen basket I see that it is nearly full. I must get down to doing some washing.

I dress, debating between gardening clobber or leisurewear. Leisurewear wins. I shall sit and meditate. It takes a long time to plan a day. There is so little choice. I could just sit. I could clean the silver. I could hoover the lounge. I could write to one of you lot. I could go shopping to Farnham or Alton or just to the village store. I could go for a walk round the village, go up as far as the church and have a chat to Maudie. I finish up back in limbo.

This seventh age is rather like waiting for a train. British Rail naturally. The train never comes. Anyway I don't know where I am going. It's a waste of time. After eight decades of making things happen I'm stuck. I am no longer of any use.

My aged bones and muscles do not respond to my motorium. My brain still functions, although even that sometimes lets me down, like when I walk all the way upstairs to get something and then can't remember what it was when I get there. I puff and blow because my bellows are worn out. I even have to seek the services of a chiropodist because my feet are now out of reach.

It's all very frustrating. I shall just put on my best face, grin from ear to ear and pour myself a rum and dry ginger which I know is not good for me.

I think of you all busily going about your daily toils and struggling for survival. I don't even have to do that.

I'm not sure that I want to.

It's all yours now kids. Take no notice of this diatribe of self pity. It's raining and there's nothing on the telly.

Cheers! All the best!

Your P.O.G.

*   *   *

3 June 1992

Dear All,

Today is Derby Day. The paper says that if I back with Ladbrokes I can save a pound. I fail to understand that because as I never back a winner how can I save a pound?

I had lunch in the Anchor at Lower Froyle. I do sometimes when I'm fed up with cooking. A young man joined me at the bar while I was enjoying my pre-lunch beer. He was dressed in the current fashion: jeans, trainers and a T-shirt emblazoned with 'Save the Rain Forests'.

He was a nice young man, gave me a polite 'Good Morning Sir' and asked me if there was a phone available. I directed him to a payphone and did a complicated transaction sorting out ten-penny pieces. He went off to make his call but was soon back seeking more ten-penny pieces. He must have been experiencing difficulties because I was well into my second pint before he returned.

Five minutes of desultory chatter passed between us before the door opened and a most attractive young lady came in, walked to the bar and kissed him. He glanced at me with a satisfied smile.

'Now that *was* worth a phone-call,' I remarked. 'Do you think I could have the phone number?'

No, I couldn't.

My attention was claimed by the Barlady. She asked me what was going to win the Derby. As I only knew the name of one runner I promptly told her that Silver Mist stood a good chance. She wrote the name on her pad. My lunch arrived and I sat quietly replenishing my spent calories.

The young man and his girl were snuggle-puffing in a secluded corner and the only other customers were two very elegant ladies enjoying their lunch at a table near the door.

It was time I went home, and as I prepared to make my exit one of the elegant ladies looked up and said, 'Excuse me, but what horse did you say would win the Derby?'

Caught on one foot for the moment I explained that I had only said that Silver Mist had a good chance and not to take my advice as a certainty.

I also embarked on one of my favourite racing stories to illustrate my point.

'I had a friend whose lucky number was seven,' I told them. 'He was the seventh son of a seventh son, he was born on the seventh of July and he went to the races on the seventh day of the month. There was a horse running in the seventh race called Seventh Heaven and he put seven pounds on it to win.'

I opened the door to let myself out as the elegant lady said anxiously, 'Did it win?'

I was nearly out of the door as I told them.

'No. It came in seventh!'

I heard their explosion of laughter as I closed the door.

I wonder if Silver Mist will win. I shall watch the telly when I get home.

I am currently into the time of the year known as 'Postcard Time'. Each morning I get a card from some exotic part of the world saying 'Wish you were here'.

This morning it was from John in Scotland. Caught three salmon. A picture of Balmoral Castle and the River Dee. X marks the spot where he caught the first one. Yesterday's card was from Ken Peet sunbathing in Ibiza. Susan favours the Lake District, Michael's card from somewhere in Hampshire and Richard sailing the high seas somewhere between Poole and France. Hermione favoured Paris. She was playing her cello in the Notre Dame. Every day I get cards. My more affluent relatives favour Venice or Hong Kong. I am pleased for them. I am not envious. I've seen and done it all. That is not quite true. I have never caught a salmon.

I am even contemplating a nostalgic pilgrimage to one of my old haunts in Pembrokeshire.

I wonder where and from whom tomorrow's card will come.

Oh well, home James and don't spare the horses.

As ever,

Your P.O.G.

* * *

5 June 1992

Dear All,

I am an Englishman. I have been English for eight decades

and now they are trying to turn me into something called a Europerson. I have no serious objections to our politicians joining the European Economic Community if it is going to assist in our financial well-being but I do not wish to become an Anglo-German, or Anglo-French or Spanish, Italian or Anglo anything else. I just wish to remain English.

I am having more than my share of problems to retain my identity from the pressures of the television programmes that are endeavouring to convert me from the Queen's English to either American or Australian.

Switching on the other day I was confronted by a large fat man wearing a ten-gallon Stetson hat, I think he was some sort of politician; at least he was haranguing a crowd of people waving flags and balloons and from his lips issued a sound which sounded something like 'Lemmetellyasumpin'.

Then from 'Down-Under' I am assailed by nasal sounds from soap operas such as *Neighbours* or *Home and Away*. Not just once a day but noon and night.

'Right on yer Jimmy boy.'

The only English one hears spoken is mostly from newsreaders, although Moira Stewart is practising to be a ventriloquist and speak without moving her lips. There is of course the occasional television play with English actors of the old school such as John Mills or Alec Guinness, and the more recent cast of the *Lovejoy* team that one can understand and enjoy. Series such as *Taggart* from north of the border need an interpreter or English sub-titles.

Our English culture is fast disappearing. Change is taking place. One only has to see the television adverts to realise the influx of outside pressures. Even our own adverts make me wonder. One in particular quite recently, I think by British Gas. It pictured a well known actress using a gas cooker during a children's tea party. It was a splendid example of how the modern English child is being educated. Table manners are now extinct.

I had better not embark on my opinion of modern music. Even my deaf ears are tortured by the cacophony of noise that emanates from these groups of berserk young natives.

11

I am old. A silly old square. Ignore me.

But I still pray that the moderns will not throw away the lovely beauty of our English heritage and replace it with raucous Americanisms.

The moral issues I will leave for a later grumble.

Be good,

As always,

P.O.G.

*   *   *

6 June 1992

Dear Georgia,

As my current morning mail consists mainly of bills and picture-postcards from wealthy relations jet-setting, as you call it, in exotic surroundings, it is most refreshing to receive a letter from someone working for their living. Thank you for enlivening my day.

I was not aware that you had returned to this green and pleasant land after your labours overseas. Your parents omitted telling me, or perhaps they did not know when I last saw them.

Life in 'Sunny old Bentley', as you term it, changes little. It is certainly not sunny as I write. In fact I have not seen the sun since Derby Day last Wednesday. My horse, Silver Mist, came third so I did not win any great fortunes but it was as I expected. Last weekend the weather was kind and our Church Flower Festival was a great success. The church looked very beautiful. Richard and Knickers who joined me for lunch in the Anchor were agreeably surprised. Not quite up to the Sunningdale standard but a splendid effort by the various village societies. I even received a blessing from the Bishop who preached on the Sunday morning. My halo remained straight for two days.

This evening I have invited your parents to join me for a celebrity concert starting with, weather permitting, a gentle stroll round the garden of Jenkyns Place. That will be followed by supper and a concert in the church featuring the Choristers

12

of Guildford Cathedral and the world famous harpist Frances Kelly. A sort of miniature Glyndebourne evening.

Your Uncle Michael and his Mary honoured me with a visit on Monday last. They came for dinner in the evening and stayed the night before returning to Somerset. I fed them one of my famous prawn salads followed by strawberries and cream. Michael assisted me in depleting the wine cellar and reminiscing about the past.

I was naturally pleased to hear of your success on the golf course and interested in all your other activities. Landsailing must be quite fun. I picture you sitting quietly on the sands in the evening making music on your panpipes. You must now be quite a virtuoso. I look forward to a recital in the near future.

Lulu was a little disappointed at Windsor. She did a good dressage and had a clear cross-country but the hard ground bruised Tarry's foot and the Vet would not pass him for the show jumping. However, she was pleased with his cross-country which has recently been her downfall.

My search for a publisher still goes on. They are the most elusive people in business. I rather feel that my poor efforts are being placed in the in-tray until the revelations of the Princess of Wales are in the bookshops. I struggle on.

Sam is avoiding the RSPB at the moment. For weeks he has been trying to catch a bird. Yesterday morning, gazing out of my lounge window, I saw a sparrow flit by about six feet from the ground. A black streak leapt from nowhere and with an overarm smash with his right paw, Sam hit the poor bird down into a bed of geraniums. He was on it in a flash and the next thing that I saw was Sam on the patio beneath the window looking up at me with a sparrow protruding from one side of his mouth and a great geranium flower from the other. His problem was how to dispose of the flower without losing the bird. I did not see the outcome. We also had a baby deer in the field but so far he has not attempted to molest it.

Your hypnotist reminded me of the war. One came to entertain the troops and after the show we invited him to the mess. One brother officer was renowned for his ability to avoid buying anyone a drink and we persuaded the Hypnotist to perform on him. Once under the influence, the Hypnotist told him to buy drinks all round. The result was hilarious. The subject was most annoyed when the 'fluence' was removed and he found that his mess bill had risen to astronomic heights.

Now I must think about lunch.

Much love from,

P.O.G.

P.S.
Felicitations from Betty.

*   *   *

8 June 1992

Dear All,

This old world of ours has come a long way since the Creation all those millions of years ago. It passed through the Neolithic Age into the Iron Age and the Steam Age, The rot started with the Industrial Revolution and was brought to a climax with the internal combustion engine in the motor car and the aeroplane. The Atomic Age is causing a spate of demonstrations from the anti-bomb enthusiasts and taking things all round with the destruction of the rain forests and the environment, We are in what might be termed, a bloody mess.

But take heart, dear children. We are now in a new age, the Age of Sex.

It dominates every section of the media. People are obsessed with sex. Ever since Lady Chatterley got involved with John Thomas one cannot pick up a book without the writer devoting at least one chapter, in an effort to outshine D H Lawrence, to vivid descriptions of sexual gymnastics. The four-letter word is on every tongue.

Sex education is taught now in our schools. I keep meaning to ask one of my grandaughters if they are expected to take 'A' levels in the subject or whether they are given practical demonstrations.

14

Looking back over my eighty years I wonder how I ever achieved my own expertise in the subject. They certainly did not instruct me at the Royal Grammar School. Perhaps I was like the late Frankie Howerd. When he was very young and they played doctors and nurses behind the garden shed and he said that he was always the one who was sent out for the bandages and when he returned he found them all playing hop-scotch. So, he grew up thinking that sex was something one did hopping on one leg.

Hardly an evening goes by without demonstrations on the television. For some unknown reason they call them adult movies. The kids are more knowledgeable than their elders. The new method of kissing also intrigues me. I always think that it looks like someone endeavouring to free a blocked waste pipe with one of those rubber suction tools. I personally have not tested it so I am not in a position to voice an opinion on this aspect of the game. I doubt now that I shall ever get the opportunity.

The health authorities also have a vested interest in the subject and even go as far as to indulge in television advertising. Be safe, use a condom. One splendid effort pictures a lady working at a condom testing bench with the caption, 'Save Margaret from redundancy. Use a condom'.

My dictionary is too old to define the word. In my day we called them 'French Letters' which I think is much nicer.

One national newspaper that I perused recently was begging for information in a list of questions relating to marital problems.

> Do either you or your partner like to have the light on or off?
>   Who initiates it? You or your partner?
>   How many times a week do you or your partner like to indulge?

The list went on and on. I wondered what response they got.

There was no instruction in sex in HM Forces. Had there been it would have probably have been done by numbers.

'On the command "One", pass the right leg over the rear arch and lower the body gently into the saddle and assume the position of attention!'

I'm getting mixed up with equitation, but on second thoughts that might not have been such a bad idea.

'Start at the walk, break into a trot, apply the aids for a steady canter and finish at a mad gallop.'

Yes, that might have been fun.

Family planning is a must. The world population is increasing beyond acceptable limits. The Archbishop is pressing the Pope to relax the laws of the Roman Catholic Church on contraception. The outcome is not yet known.

It will probably start a 'condom price-war'. Actually contraception is nothing new. We considered the need fifty years ago. We were introduced to a product which, if I remember correctly, had the trade name of 'Rendells'.

For a short space of time Kathleen and I proved its efficiency until one morning at breakfast when I found one of these small tablets in my pyjama pocket. I decided that it would not be wise to risk it in our next engagement so I tossed it onto the fire. There was a loud explosion and a great sheet of flame shot up the chimney. As this contraceptive device was used internally by the female partner, my wife immediately had visions of blowing up or catching fire if we continued to use them. My suggestion that I kept a fire extinguisher beside the bed was not accepted.

I waffle on.

With seventeen grandchildren it is quite obvious that my own personal family received no instruction in the subject but of course the grandchildren will be more enlightened.

They get taught in school.

There is a lot more to this subject but I think that I have said enough.

If you can't be good, be careful. Use a condom.

All my love,

P.O.G.

* * *

Dear All,

I woke up today to a glorious June morning and decided that it was a day for meditation which is another word for idleness.

Then I remembered that I had to go to Farnham to collect my new suit that was being altered. I dashed off early so that I would be able to park and just made it before the mass of weekend shoppers arrived.

I puffed my way along to the Tailors threading through the motley throng of people. I am always amazed at the variety of apparel that people favour. The younger generation seem determined to look as scruffy as they can. Girls with cut-off jeans all frayed at the hem, grubby T-shirts emblazoned with a variety of slogans and generally hair resembling an O'Cedar mop. Women with great bulging behinds encased in skin-tight jeans, pecking along on six-inch heels looking rather like big fat broody hens. Most young men appear naked from the waist up, and most of the next generation appear pregnant with huge bulging stomachs, while the elders of the nation, like myself, totter along in our pre-war outfits. My new suit is the first one I've bought for fifteen years. I think that I only bought it out of spite. I doubt if I shall ever have occasion to wear it. To church perhaps.

My tailor was pleased to see me anyway, and found a chair for me to sit on so that I might recover my breath. He should have been pleased to see me. My cheque for something in excess of £300 brought a satisfied smile to his lips.

Extracting myself from the carpark I drove back home again more firmly convinced than ever that the speed limit had been increased to 90 mph. It is always with a sense of relief to return the car to its garage.

I said hello to Sam who asked for a little refreshment and seemed satisfied with a dish of duck and liver Whiskers.

The cat food manufacturers must think that we are all stupid.

Duck and liver, salmon and trout, chicken and kidney, beef and liver. I wish someone would do a television investigation into these gourmet pet foods and show us how they arrive at such exotic titles.

Sam seemed more or less content although the look he gave me was eloquent enough to convince me that if it hadn't have been so hot outside he would have gone hunting for a mouse. Bone idle.

Beginning to feel somewhat disconsolate, I poured myself a medicinal Planters Punch and sat quietly deciding what I might do next.

Refreshed, I thought that a stroll round the village might put me in a better frame of mind. Go up to the church and ensure that Maudie was behaving herself and not turning in her grave. She did last month when someone put plastic flowers there. She was allergic to plastic flowers.

Walking along the quiet country lanes in June always revives me, especially if they have been haymaking. The hedgerows are a blaze of wild flowers enhanced with empty Coca-Cola tins, cigarette packets and empty plastic bags that once contained Walkers Crisps. Our hedgerows and ditches are developing into another means of advertising. I met no one.

I relaxed on the seat under the church wall and closed my eyes. It was very peaceful. Maudie was not in the mood for conversation so I went into the church to have a chat with the Boss-man. I said a prayer for all you lot and a tiny one for myself. I don't think I'm in His good books at the moment. Most of my personal wants He completely ignores. I sometimes think that the line is always engaged. Anyway He probably thinks that I don't need anything. I suppose really I don't. He's got more than enough on His plate if the BBC World News is accurate. I said 'thanks anyway', and we parted on good terms.

I walked back home past the doctor's surgery. By the number of cars in the carpark it seems that the health of the village is in a sorry state. Perhaps they only go there to read the magazines in the waiting room.

The house was as I left it. Sam opened one eye and immediately went back to sleep.

18

My own mind now drifts into the 'What shall I have for lunch?' stage. Lamb chop, new potatoes, broad beans followed by strawberries and cream. Perhaps another Planters Punch might give me the incentive.

Love in mint sauce,

P.O.G.

* * *

14 June 1992

My Dear Children,

It is a perfect June morning and I have just returned from early morning Communion. I so much prefer the old St James' Service to the modern sung Eucharist and the family one. Old habits die hard.

So today might well be a good time to reflect on my views about the Church and religion as it has affected me.

Mercy Elizabeth started me off as soon as I was old enough to learn the *Lord's Prayer*. To begin with she would stand over me as I knelt beside my bed to ensure that I said it correctly and always ended up with, 'Bless Mum and Dad and Hilda and all kind friends.' I always had to kneel beside my bed except when there was ice on the windows and then I would be allowed to get into bed first. I rapidly became fluent and could probably say the *Lord's Prayer* faster than anyone.

At the age of eleven when I started at the Royal Grammar School and education became more complicated, I began to add, 'and please help me at school tomorrow'. I was never conscious of Him sending a Pentecostal Wind to assist me with my French and Latin and I began to think that the Lord was not a great deal better at algebra than I was.

At Sunday School I received a sound knowledge of the Old Testaments with favourites such as David and Goliath and Daniel in the Lions' Den. I knew the Ten Commandments by heart although nowadays they are reduced to two:

'Love the Lord thy God with all thy heart, and with all thy soul, and with all thy mind and with all thy strength. This is the

19

first Commandment. And the second is like, namely this: Thou shalt love thy neighbour as thyself. There is no other Commandment greater than these. On these two Commandments hang all the Law and Prophets'.

I think that one is apt to forget the other 'Thou shalt nots'.

And so I, by the time I left school, was a fully fledged paid-up member of the Church of England and the fear of God was firmly instilled into me.

I don't think it was long before I went behind His back to savour some of the delights of wickedness and vice and discovered that the 'wrath of God' was not too unpleasant.

Mind you, I still kept looking over my shoulder to see if He was looking but He probably did not consider that a wicked half-pint of beer in the Seven Stars would justify excommunication.

Again, Mercy Elizabeth still had her eye on me and I was not allowed to back-slide on Sundays.

My sinning was kept to a minimum.

Then in the Army, although profanity became a common language, I was kept too busy and too short of money to indulge or get involved in the 'fleshpots of the world'. Again there were no dens of iniquity at Tidworth and Regimental Church Parade, and Padre's Hour each week kept the Lord in sight.

I think that it was in York that I really had my first serious thoughts about my religion. I remember a day when I felt particularly depressed. About what I don't know, but I wandered into the great Minster. The organist was practising and as I sat quietly at the rear of this great cathedral, it seemed as if the vibrations from the glorious sound were invading my very being. It was a strange sensation. Almost as if the music was telling me that there was a presence there. I only know I walked out feeling elated and that my depression was gone.

Then I met and courted Kathleen. Religion paid a great part in our courtship. Most evenings we did our snuggle-puffing in the porch of Flore Church – one could not improve on that. Then there was our marriage and the vows we made that kept us constant during the difficult years of separation when I was in India and the war years, the arrival of the children; Sunday picnic on the beach but not until after church; Granny Page, whose devout faith helped us over difficult times; nearly twenty-five years and churches all over the world – until the tragedy that took her from me. It was the faith that we had found that helped me over that awful time.

Then Theresa Mona. She too, although in a different way to Kathleen, found help from her beliefs. We were both so lucky with the men of the Church that befriended and helped us. The Rev. John Marcon; the Rev. Graham Barnet; the Rev. Peter Shaw in Alderney; the Rev. Gerald Gardner-Brown at Lydbury North; the Rev. Herbert Thomas in Kingsland – a saint if ever there was one; and then the canons and clergy of Gloucester Cathedral until the Rev. Bill Rogers, who was to care for her in her last years of pain and illness.

And now that I am on my own in this seventh age I still believe and gather strength from my prayers. I still say the *Lord's Prayer* very quickly and sometimes when it gets automatic I find myself asking Him for help at school tomorrow. Then I say sorry and start again. I am old enough to be allowed to criticise the Church. I don't always agree with what they say or do.

Archbishop Runcie was often a subject for disagreement. To us he seldom seemed to give a firm directive. When Sam sat surveying the field from his favourite spot on the fence at the end of the garden Theresa would say, 'There's Sam doing a Runcie again.'

Lay-people that say the prayers in church mumble in an inaudible fashion so that I find myself looking heavenwards and saying, 'I hope You can hear what and who he is praying for because I can't.'

The reading of the Scriptures is another of my pet subjects for criticism. So few people read well. To listen to the Reverend John Marcon reading from the Bible was sheer pleasure and he would make me cross when he allowed his church warden to do it for him. The man was completely inarticulate. Why do they do it? John Marcon said that it was because he did not want to offend his wealthy church warden. 'Rubbish', I said.

Fire and brimstone from the Pulpit is a thing of the past. It's all 'love-thy-neighbour' now. A few 'Thou shalt nots' might do a little more good.

I expect I'm just old. Graham Barnet once called me a Dogmatic old Army Officer. Perhaps I am but remember my children that when I move on I shall ask for dispensation to come back and do a little haunting.

So, as little Orphan Annie said:

> Be mindful of what yer say and do,
> yer better mind yer parents too,
> and yer teachers fond and dear,
> and cherish them that loves yer
> and dry the orphan tear,
> and 'elp the poor and needy ones that clusters all about,
> er the Goblins'll get yer if yer don't watch out.

I've waffled on again.
God Bless. Forgive your,
P.O.G.

P.S.
For Katharine.

Dear Katharine,

I understand that you are having difficulty with a professed Atheist.

There is no such person as an Atheist. It is merely a term that they use to excuse themselves when they break God's instructions.

I have met many such men. I immediately ask them what their 'Christian' name is and I am told that it is 'George', or 'Frederick', or 'James', and then I ask them how an Atheist can have a 'Christian' name?

It is the one thing in their lives that they can *never* change. It is indelibly printed on their forehead for the duration of their existence in this world. And the hereafter, it is like having an army number. They can never change it. They can change their surname by Deed Poll, but never their Christian name!

In my early days in the Army when Church Parade was compulsory, all other denominations, Non-Conformists, Jews, Roman Catholics etc. – and Atheists, had to parade in the rear of the Regiment before it marched off. The other denominations were marched to their respective places of worship and the Atheists reported to the Provost Sergeant for Fatigues. It was surprising how quickly they became C of Es after a few hours cleaning out the latrines!

Maybe you could try that method out in your effort at conversion.

Anyway I can only suggest that you really ask him why. I suspect that it is an excuse to use you without feeling any guilt.

No love is possible without belief. It is merely a physical expression of the body which succumbs to the excitement of hormones that get out of control. It can never last.

Tell your Nigel, or whatever his 'Christian' name is, that he is a phoney. I said at the start of my letter that now I am old I can say what I think.

Be good and God Bless.

Your affectionate P.O.G

*   *   *

7 July 1992

Dear Hermione,

It was with a sense of relief that I picked your letter up from my doormat this morning. A refreshing change from the endless demands of HM Government and the masses of junk mail telling me that I am now £50,000 better off and if I return the slip in seven days, I qualify for a mystery prize.

Regarding your query about a present as I enter the age of the octogenarian, I can only suggest the 'Elixir of Life' or a new pair of bellows to assist me in puffing my way round the village. I can think of nothing that I need although I am getting to the end of the shaving soap that you sent me last year, Yardley's Black Label.

I watched little of Wimbledon except the finals. I enjoyed the men's final and was pleased that the Graf girl beat the grunting American.

I was sorry to hear that you had retired from the church choir. It cannot possibly be as good without you and as for Anne and her Karate, I can only suggest a change of diet. I watched a programme the other evening which proved that the aggressiveness in the modern 'little monster' was entirely due to dietry problems. You should write to the BBC for details! I am sure too that your 'Scholar of the Year' will soon be gracing the ancient halls of Cambridge.

Do you intend to go into high finance when you have got a First in your business studies course? Do you graduate and get a cap and gown? Georgia did at the termination of her physical training college. She wears it while teaching abseiling and golf.

I am sorry to hear that Roger's wheels have at last expired. Mine, being a Lancer, still canters along albeit more slowly than of yore. It has spasms when it suddenly wants to race away and then subsides with a gentle sigh of exhaustion. We returned on Sunday from a 647-mile nostalgic pilgrimage covering the last two weeks. I am hoping that a period of rest and quiet may encourage her to survive the rest of the year. She is certainly somewhat fragile after venturing into the wilds of Wales.

I started off with my fingers crossed stopping first in Gloucester where I had lunch with some old friends that I had not seen for thirty years. That was a very pleasant interlude before I went on to Ross-on-Wye where I luxuriated in a four-star hotel. I spent two days doing the rounds of all our old friends, had tea in Crocketts and took some photographs. They have looked after it very well and made very few changes apart from a spiral staircase from the dining room to that room below. The trees in the garden have all grown to unbelievable heights. Maudie would have been proud to see her handiwork looking so beautiful.

After three days I continued quietly on to Pembroke where I had booked a room at the King's Arms. The same landlord that I knew from my Military days. They gave me a great welcome and encouraged me to imbibe too much wine. Harriet and Bob from Warren Farm joined me almost before I had finished the first bottle. It was a real welcome. The only thing missing was the red carpet.

I spent the next few days at Castlemartin visiting my old haunts and so many old friends that I had not seen for thirty years. The little church at Warren, where Kathleen is buried, has been rebuilt and refurbished by the Germans stationed on the Ranges. I took lots of photographs, had gorgeous steak and kidney pie in the farmhouse and let Harriet drive me to Angle where we sat on the beach licking Cornettos. Then on to Freshwater West and the other bays of my halcyon days. I visited the camp where the Colonel is a colleague of John's and was taken on a tour of inspection and proudly shown all the improvements that have been made since I ran it – all computers and gadgets. I did the same job with a map and two Chinagraph pencils. However, it was all very interesting and the lunch in the officers' mess was well up to standard.

You may remember the Davies family from the days that you stayed there. They are all well over thirty now. Hugh is married with three children and working the farm with Robin. Harriet and Bob have retired to the Old Nurses House and Richard is a non-productive attachment. Kathleen is married to a mathematics master at Pembroke Grammar School! She had one boy who I was unable to converse with due either to my inability to speak Welsh or his complete dumbness. Altogether I had a very enjoyable visit and I did consider going AWOL but thought better of it and turned eastwards thinking to stop in Monmouth where I quenched my thirst, had a pub lunch and decided to push on to my aged sister in Minehead. That part of my travels was a nightmare. That is if one can have a nightmare at 1400 hours. From the Severn Bridge at Chepstow the M5 was a truly frightening experience. Did you know that the speed limit has been increased to 90 mph on the motorways? At least I assume it has because that is the speed that everyone was doing as they passed me.

Sister Hilda, now eighty-seven years old, was pleased to see me and I spent the last few days of my tour gathering my strength for my return to Bentley. A geriatric cure; I did find the remains of a bottle of gin in her cupboard and a small tonic. It had probably been there since the end of the War. South Africa.

The rains came. I drove to Angela's at Tollard Royal up a river flowing through miles of roadworks. I spent more time at traffic lights than I did motoring but I eventually made it. Then naturally it was all horses. I had to inspect all the new acquisitions and give my expert opinion. I watched the instruction and even mounted a quiet mare to have my picture taken. Angela pressed the button and the resulting photo finds me with only half my head.

I did not prolong my visit and by early afternoon on Sunday I was back in Bentley luxuriating in a much needed bath. Sam welcomed me as usual with open claws.

I am now recuperating.

I enclose the programme of an evening in June when I invited Richard and Nicola over for a semi-Glyndebourne evening. It was most successful. We had never had supper in a churchyard before. We used an ancient tombstone as a table on which to rest our wine glasses. The concert was splendid so I am told. Most of it was beyond my musical knowledge and so I could not in all honesty voice an opinion.

Now I really must stop. Forgive me for using this machine but at least you should be able to read it.

As ever,

Your very ancient P.O.G.

P.S.

I was sorry to hear that Jersey is again under the jackboot. British this time, not German.

*   *   *

24 July 1992

Dear All,

In two days time I shall have been in this vale of tears for seventy-nine years and according to my 'Horror-scope' the future does not look promising. The sun, Venus and Mercury together in Leo seem to be putting me on the spot. However, the mighty planet Saturn passing through my opposite sign of Aquarius warns me to remember that whatever my dilemma, feelings come and go, but principles remain fast.

If you can make any sense out of that please let me know.

Looking back over the years, I become distinctly morbid. I try to think what I have done to make the world a better place and I come to the conclusion 'nothing'.

I have allowed an empire to be frittered away. I was born just before the War to end all wars and two decades later saw it all again in another holocaust started by the same nation as before. My own feeble efforts did little to end this stupidity and merely wasted six years of my life.

The rest of the time I have just wandered round the world helping to bog things up a little further.

I taught the Iraqis the elementary principles of Tank Warfare using obsolete Churchill Mk VIII tanks, sold to them by my government. So I helped to set the wheels, or tracks, in motion for them to invade Saudi Arabia some forty years later and involve us in The Gulf War.

In the interim period the Germans became our best friends and Allies in a 'Cold War' against the threat of the Red Peril. All that happened then was a massive airlift to Berlin to feed the beleaguered citizens. The Russians built their Berlin Wall and the Arms Race began with America and Russia stockpiling nuclear missiles.

Britain was slowly going down hill and getting more confused with the passing years. Our politicians waffle on.

It seems that the largest parts of our industries were being taken over by the Americans, Japanese and oil-wealthy Arabs.

James did nothing to stop the rot.

Now it is too late. He has allowed the politicians to sell the country out to something called the European Economic Community so that it is now impossible to apply for a British passport. They are now Europassports. James is no longer an

27

Englishman but a Euroman.

And the news gets worse daily. Our politicians assure me that the Recession is ending and one can be assured by their happy smiling faces that this is so when one watches them shaking hands in Brussels and posing for the cameras.

Public spending 'must be curbed'. So what do they do? They pass a resolution in Westminster increasing their allowances to £40 000 per annum. This is probably needed to cover their 'little bits on the side'.

James in bewildered. His faith in our national leaders is shattered. Their morals are said to be 'their private lives'. To James it seems that they set a bloody awful example to the rank and file.

So what can he do as he enters his seventy-ninth year? He is told that he should remedy the problem by getting on his knees.

Perhaps it would if everyone followed suit but it seems that there are only a few voices in the wilderness.

The Church is a confused mess anyway.

Will James just pass the problems on to someone else?

Richard, John, Michael, Angela, Susan, Hermione and all their families. Should he just leave it all to them now?

Perhaps if they stop to think and examine their own lives they will not make the same mistakes as James.

No. James will still try to make amends. Say what he feels is right. Criticise where he feels that it is necessary and not mind being called a silly, dogmatic old fool.

What a lot of codswallop I have waffled.

It is time that I went for an amble round the village. I shall have a look at Granny Maudie and have a quiet chat with my Boss up at St Mary's.

God Bless England and down with the Euroclots.

As ever,

Your P.O.G.

*   *   *

Dear All,

Another birthday has flown under the bridge and how I survived it can only be put down to Divine assistance.

Richard, Nicola, John, Taffy, Angela, David and a host of grandchildren did their utmost to arrange my immediate demise.

Fortunately I started the day by going to the eight o'clock Communion Service and pray for strength and patience.

It was granted. Betty joined me later during the morning to start the celebrations with a Jamaican coffee which we drank quietly sitting in the garden. Richard and Nicola arrived at 2.15 p.m., their melodious voices joined in the time honoured 'Happy Birthday to Grandad'. Nicola presented me with a parcel suitably wrapped in Happy Birthday paper which was even more secure than Fort Knox and quite burglar proof. I was exhausted before I uncovered it. To my surprise, you'll never guess, a bottle!

The label described it as:

The Elixir of Life.

P.O.G.

The instructions warned me not to exceed the laid down dosage, to drink it only in the presence of friends and to keep it out of the reach of Michael and Hermione.

As I am devoid of friends and Michael and Hermione are safely out of reach it seems improbable that I shall ever be able to test this magical potion.

Leaving Betty in charge of Sam and No. 17, I was forced into an automobile and driven off down the A31 and was able to notice that we passed through Winchester and Salisbury. We eventually entered a dangerous collection of what was obviously the married quarters of the remains of Her Majesty's Army. There we met a colonel disguised in civilian clobber; very ancient jeans with a bony knee visible beneath a large hole in the leg, and two ladies similarly attired, but with no holes in the legs.

Believe it or not but it was my long lost son John with Taffy his wife and Rachel one of my beautiful grandaughters.

What a welcome! I was put into a chair while my guardians began to talk all at the same time. I tried to adjust my electric ears but was unable to follow their vigorous conversation. Eventually I was fed with a portion of chocolate cake and a liquid that I was told was tea. I obviously looked as though I would not survive because my son forced a large gin and tonic down my parched throat.

I survived and at 7 p.m. I was again secured in the front seat of Richard's car and strapped down with a belt across my chest. This time we were following John, who had Taffy and Rachel with him, and I noticed the change in terrain. We were driving into the depths of rural England. I became aware of familiar hedgerows. I saw a sign, Tollard Royal, and knew that I was being delivered to the horse people.

We arrived. I was released and then enveloped in the arms of my favourite daughter. Angela almost suffocated me with birthday kisses. My arms were nearly shaken off as David and Justin grasped my hands, and then Katie and Lulu took over and began forcing some strange alcoholic fruit salad down my throat. I was forced into yet another chair. Deluged with envelopes containing an array of greeting cards, parcels were poured into my lap and I was left to delve into all these gifts while a confused cacophony of voices all talking at once echoed from the rafters.

It was the start of a great birthday feast.

How Angela found the time to prepare such a sumptuous table of gourmet food I shall never know but it was certainly a magnificent sight. It was also not long before everyone was busy with knives, forks and spoons devouring these delicacies. Lulu, I noticed as she sat cross legged on the floor, had a whole mountain of food on her plate. My mother would have been horrified at the way they were all talking with their mouths full. The noise was unbelievable. I could distinguish Richard's hearty guffaws above the delicate pipings of the ladies. David seemed to be continually walking round with a wine bottle replenishing empty glasses.

Occasionally someone would arrive to sit by me in an effort to converse but they soon got frustrated when I gave them completely wrong answers to their questions. My hearing aids are apt to be somewhat confusing in multi-gatherings.

However, it was sheer pleasure to see such a large gathering of my family all together and enjoying each other's company. And it was all for my benefit.

I am a very lucky man.

Time goes so quickly and it seemed that I was soon being assisted into John's car deluged with kisses and handshaking farewells. I was to spend the night with Army protection.

Then it was all over and I was tucked up in bed after reminding John to wake me with a cup of tea.

He did. It was a strange feeling to be awakened by a uniformed figure after all these years. I recovered slowly under ministrations from Taffy who was to transport me back home. She looked so completely fresh and alive. She had also been doing all the driving the night before.

I felt very much the way that I looked when I saw myself in the mirror while shaving. Ghastly.

And now it was the twenty-seventh. Theresa Mona's birthday. I reflected back over the years that we had celebrated together.

I felt a little sad that she had not been with me. How she would have loved to have the family all around her.

Taffy drove in truly professional perfection and I directed her to the Anchor Inn at Lower Froyle where we were to lunch and drink Theresa's health.

Rosemary behind the bar was surprised to see me with yet another such attractive lady. 'How do you find them?' I assured her that it was my good looks and incredible charm.

We enjoyed a quiet meal, toasted Theresa Mona with beer and then it was all over.

Taffy left me in my garden and drove off back to her John.

My birthday was all over. It had been a splendid two days that will always be remembered.

I wonder what this eightieth year will bring?

Keep your fingers crossed all of you.

Thank you for a wonderful birthday.

Your P.O.G.

* * *

7 August 1992

Dear Nicola,

It was strange that you should have asked me about *The Village* because I have just listened to the BBC's latest episode and I have also read Mr Nigel Farrell's book. I must, in all honesty, admit that I have not been impressed by the book or the broadcasts.

It does not reflect the village of Bentley that I have come to know and love. I have every admiration for the few people that form the basis of his work. Margaret and Hilda Evans are truly sterling people whom I am proud to call friends. Mr and Mrs Grove at the Gardens Farm are the salt of the earth and old Walter Sherfield has, without any shadow of doubt, over his long life contributed so much to making Bentley the village that Mr Farrell endeavours to portray.

And the same applies to the other villagers that he describes but I do not think that walking around with a microphone recording odd conversations in odd places does the village justice.

I appreciate the magnitude of the task that Mr Farrell has attempted but I feel that he has not found the heart of the real Bentley. He had to start somewhere and I suppose that Glade Farm was as good as anywhere but it is not Bentley. The whole project would be beyond me.

Perhaps I could in my amateurish way give you my story of Bentley and its people.

As you may remember, due to old age and ill health, Theresa Mona and I had to move from our beloved Crocketts on the edges of the Forest of Dean to somewhere, defined by our children as near to civilisation, and estate agents in Farnham were asked to find a house fulfilling my requirements.

The priorities were that it had to be a village. Medical care would be essential and within easy reach and a village shop and Post Office in walking distance. A church and a pub were a must. Public transport should be available against the time when we

32

could no longer drive ourselves.

Weller Eggar found us No. 17 Eggars Field. It was a near perfect choice. It, although not a Crocketts, fulfilled our needs.

Mr Farrell, in his book regrettably refers to the estate as the place of the commuter people who drive off each morning and return late in the evening and are not really part of the village. He is so very wrong.

I am not a Hampshire man but I was born just a few miles over the border in Surrey, so in a way it was like coming back home. I remember in my youth upsetting the peace and quiet of Bentley as I roared through it on my motorcycle.

It was June. Theresa had written in her diary: 'They tell me that I have only three months left.' July passed, August came and we were into September. The medical estimate was wrong and although we both knew that it was borrowed time, Theresa was with me for almost three more years, not just three months. It would not have been possible without the care and attention she had from Doctor Jonathan Moore and his colleague Doctor Sword. It seemed that they gave her a new lease of life. The District Nurse, Sister Eileen Rawlings and her team of nurses were wonderful. Theresa, during those last months of her life could not have had better attention anywhere in the world. The Rector, the Reverend Bill Rogers, never once failed to call each week. He became a great friend and comforter. He brought Communion to her each month and his visits were an inspiration and certainly helped her to bear the sickness and pain and to remain brave and cheerful.

Neighbours too, in this so called Commuter Estate, were kindness itself. Betty Horlock from No. 21 was always to hand when I needed help. She had lost her own husband the Christmas after we took up residence, but she became a great friend in need. Mrs Kay Mason, over eighty herself, always found time to come and chat, bring flowers and a cheerful presence. Bentley and its people were good to us both.

When the end came and Theresa was laid to rest at the beautiful old church of St Mary's I was never to forget the support that I received. Three things remain etched in my mind of that day. The address by the Rector, the singing of her favourite hymns by all our children and friends old and new, and the team of six nurses who had cared for her and came up to kiss my cheek at the graveside.

And now, in the three years since Theresa died, I have learned more of the people of Bentley. It is a great English village with a great cross-section of personalities. Rich people, not so rich and even poor, but all of a oneness.

In this my eightieth year, I take my daily constitutional exercise around the village stopping every hundred yards or so to take deep breaths to help my worn out bellows or talk to whoever I am fortunate enough to meet.

At the end of Eggars Field where it meets School Lane, I make my first stop and watch the children racing around the playground. I never fail to be amused at the crescendo of noise that their shrill voices make as they indulge in their various games – the future villagers of Bentley. And I wonder what legacy I am helping to leave them.

I walk on up School Lane and probably meet my old friend Arthur Farrow also out for his constitutional walk. We discuss our various infirmities and tell one another what a shocking state the world is in. The hill up to the church gets steeper every day. I stop every hundred yards and do my deep breathing exercises. I eventually make it to the churchyard where I stroll round and have a chat to Theresa and invariably find Mr Bonner or Mr Hollingdale cutting the grass. We chat and I learn something new about the village. In the church itself I sit for a few moments and meditate. If it happens to be Wednesday Mrs Holingdale will be cleaning. I have got into the habit of carrying a bag of peardrops which she always appreciates. Mrs Honor Seymour who I sometimes meet exercising her Jack Russells can never remember my name and refers to me as 'The Peardrop Man'.

Mr Farrell did not do justice to the Village Flower Festival or the splendid Celebrity Concert. I believe I told you about that memorable 'Mini-Glyndebourne' evening in my last letter.

Continuing along the top towards Jenkyn Place I admire the roses and flowers surrounding John of Pease Cottage. It is always a blaze of colour. Down the footpath under the wall in Hole Lane I pass the doctor's surgery. By the number of cars in the carpark I assess the health of the village. Doctor Moore, by the look of things, is having a very busy morning. On past the Memorial Hall and along the main road to the village shop. I cringe at the incessant stream of traffic and wonder whether the by-pass will ever materialise.

In the shop I fall into Sheila's arms, exhausted. She smooths my perspiring brow and has been known to find a stool for me to sit on and recover.

The shop ladies are wonderful. Sheila, Shirley, Karen and Sue always give me a welcome and I have never known them to be without a laugh or a smile. Sally, the mainstay of the shop and the Post Office, is without a doubt the best postmistress in England. She too is never cross or without a smile and a cheerful word. Terry, the van salesman always makes my day if he is in the shop. He can always provide a certain good tip for Ascot or Goodwood.

I complete my walk up through the Commuter Estate past Nick in his workshop where he is looking after the needs of all our motor cars. I meet Alastair being perambulated by his mother. I never think she looks old enough to have a baby son. Alastair is just over one year old and the smile he gives me is like a ray of sunshine. I meet Thomas with his mum, sometimes his grandmother. He too gives a happy grin. I met a Sue the other day with a brand-new daughter, Claudia. There are others too. Young women who are never too busy to stop and chat to an old man out for a walk. These are the new villagers and the future.

Back home I find Betty has mowed my grass. I make two long mint juleps and we sit and count our blessings.

I must stop. There is so much more. So many more wonderful people. Perhaps another letter, another day.

Be good to one another.

Your P.O.G.

* * *

Dear All,

I am despondent. It is raining and a howling wind is playing havoc in the garden. Sam is also fed up and curled up sulking on the swingseat.

My mail this morning merely comprised a bank statement and another rejection slip. At least the bank statement showed a credit balance albeit somewhat depleted.

The rejection slip at least gave a reason. I quote:

> Autobiographies and Memoirs are very hard to publish successfully without a name to back them. Unfair, as work such as yours is often more interesting than that of so called celebrities . . . *Blah! Blah! Blah!* . . .We suggest . . . .

How do I become a celebrity if they don't publish?

Sally in the Post Office suggests that I become a 'streaker' but I hardly think that I would be able to streak fast enough. Perhaps robbing the Post Office in the nude might get me a spot in *The Sun.*

I have now sent it all off to Publisher No. 6 with a slight alteration. I have called it, 'The story of a *famous unknown* soldier. Percy Verance is now my new name.

I suppose I should be grateful that I am not on a camping holiday like my new neighbours.

What a depressing world it has all become. Beer is now £16 a gallon and milk dearer than petrol. Mind you, I don't think I would like petrol in my morning tea.

I, like most of my contemporaries, still think in terms of pounds, shillings and pence. Five shillings of old money to post one silly little letter! A few years ago I could have posted twenty-five letters for that with only one class and deliveries morning and afternoon.

It was decimalisation that did it. All they have to do is move that little dot about and £5.00 so easily becomes £50.00. I am told that when Inflation is at a controlled level things will be better. I always understood that inflation was to blow things up like bicycle tyres and hot-air balloons. There's enough hot air going up to waste over Westminster and Brussels to make British Gas or the electricity boards obsolete.

What a good old grumble I'm having. It doesn't make me feel any better.

James, you must smile and thank your lucky stars that you are not in Bosnia, Ethiopia, South Africa or anywhere else on this strife-ridden planet but in dear, good old Bentley.

And now as I think it is time to go and put the kettle on I see that the sun is shining again.

Hooray!

Keep your fingers crossed for your Famous Unknown,

P.O.G.

*   *   *

16 August 1992

Dear All,

My mind for some unknown reason has drifted on to charity. Faith, hope and charity and the greatest of these is charity.

I remember, when I was a small boy still at school, how the tramps, gypsies and hawkers put their secret signs on the front gates of houses to let any of their kind who came after them know that the occupants were an easy touch or whether they had a bad-tempered dog. The tramps of course would spend the night at the workhouse where they could always get a meal. Signs such as 'No Hawkers. No Circulars' adorned many gates.

I am sure that nowadays the same system applies to the good people that go from door to door collecting for charities. Somewhere in the front of No. 17 Eggars Field there must be a sign that tells them that old James is always good for a sub. It seems that hardly a day goes by without some 'do-gooder' ringing my bell and shaking a tin with a slot in the top for contributions.

I am a collector of badges to stick or display on my person to inform everyone what a generous bloke I am.

37

I have stickers from the RSPCA, the RSPB and the RSPCC. Sam of course is a paid-up member of the Cats Protection League but he has no time for the RSPB. Birds to him are legitimate food. He also has no respect for mice. He is not particularly fond of children either – grown-ups too for that matter.

Yesterday I subscribed to the Phyllis Tuckwell Hospice. I received another sticker. All in a good cause. The Royal Lifeboat Association presented me with a little lifeboat to pin on my coat and Cancer Research sent me a catalogue in preparation for Christmas.

The Spastics Society leaves a great bag for me to put a variety of oddments in that I no longer have a use for, so that they can sell them in their shop in the town. The Spastics Society always reminds me of Mrs Lobb, Kathleen's cleaning lady at Lulworth. She informed me that her husband was employed by The Customs and Exiles and as she shook her collecting box under my nose she said that it was in aid of 'The Plastic Children'.

Christian Aid Week brings forth another bevy of good ladies ready to take advantage of my generous nature.

Help the Aged I always think is carrying it just a little too far when one is on the verge of being an octogenarian. But I still with a sigh put my hand into my pocket. James you're mad.

The Church Restoration Fund is continually thinking up new ideas to remove me of my surplus wealth and that is without my monthly 'alms and oblations' that the Lord himself expects of me.

The Salvation Army knows perfectly well that I can never turn them away empty handed after all the cups of tea they made for me in the remotest parts of the British Empire before we gave it all away and the 16th/5th The Queen's Royal Lancers Benevolent Fund just gives me a direct order.

'You will donate or else . . . .'

Theresa, in a rash moment inveigled me into making out a banker's order to become a Friend of Gloucester Cathedral and I noticed yesterday on my bank statement that I am still subscribing yearly. James, you really are mad.

Remembrance Sunday will soon be looming up and I shall be

forking out for my sixtieth poppy. I could work out exactly how many if I put my mind to it. That is one that I could not get out of.

There are others of course but I get so confused that I can't remember them all. I don't count the pleas from ITV or the BBC who periodically have their Telethon and Red Nose Marathons, or the Appeals on Sunday evenings for a seemingly different cause each week.

Someone once told me that charity begins at home and I can tell you, from personal experience, that with six children and seventeen grandchildren, not counting sisters, brothers, maiden-aunts and close friends, birthdays and Christmas tend to strain the old exchequer and the brain.

Greeting cards produced by every charity under the sun. A large portion of that of course can be blamed on to Theresa Mona. And now that August is here the shops will soon be shouting 'Buy early for Christmas'. In fact I saw one display of cards this morning.

What with Save the Whales, Porpoises, Gorillas, Elephants, The Rain Forests – and the world in general all clamouring for funds one needs to be a Paul Getty which I am not. I remember the days when on the last Friday in the month I would sit down and make cheques out for all the bills and turn to Theresa Mona and say, 'We've got three and thrupence left. What would you like to do with it?'

She in a flash would say, 'You can buy me a pint of beer over at the Tichbourne.' She would be unlucky in this day and age. Three shillings and three pence, 16p today, would hardly fill a wineglass with beer.

So dear children, this letter should explain to you why I am so in need of charity. A collecting box with the label 'JAMES' BENEVOLENT FUND' is now on the hall table ready for your next visits.

Melba once said of me, 'James, you are too generous.'

But I can't help it. I am a sucker for anyone shaking a collecting box.

Perhaps like Abou Ben Adhem (may his tribe increase), I shall wake one night from a deep dream of peace and see an angel writing in a book of gold and I shall say to him, 'I pray thee then, write me as one that loves his fellow men.' I wonder if the angel would come back the next night as he did to dear old Abou Ben Adhem?

I doubt that old James' name would lead all the rest.

As you know, my Society for the Suppression of Mirth and the Promotion of Misery is still open for membership. I might take this opportunity of reminding Georgia, Frederick and James that they have not paid their annual subscriptions for the last five years.

Love in begging bowls,

Your penniless P.O.G.

* * *

18 August 1992

Dear Children and Friends,

I read statistics somewhere recently stating that the average person spends a third of their life in bed. If that is correct, and I am an average person, it means that give or take a year or two I have spent twenty-six years in the old Charpoy. That is a lot of beds in a lot of different places. Mind you, bed is one of my favourite places. I've had some good times in bed and not what you lecherous lot are thinking.

When I was a small boy bed was my favourite place. I could pull the sheet up over my head and enter a world that was all mine, that no one else could enter. A world of fantasy. I was the best fencer in the world. The Three Musketeers were novices with a sword compared with me. I was infinitely superior to Robin Hood with the long-bow and that is saying something. With a Colt 45 I could put six shots into the ace of spades at twenty-five yards. Even Billy the Kid could not do that.

I rescued innumerable damsels-in-distress by flinging them across my saddle-bow and galloping off in the style of young Lochinvar. I rode Grand National winners and consorted with famous heroes like Bulldog Drummond. My fantasy world naturally depended on what I was reading at the time. If it was

40

Jeffrey Farnoll I would be giving advice to Jasper Shrigg and his Bow Street Runners. As I grew older Dornford Yates took over and I adventured with Berry and Co.

Then I had to leave that wonderful world and grow up.

Beds grew harder. The Army 'biscuits' that His Majesty provided were not the ultimate in luxury but I was told that they were good for me. Anyway, I had little choice and generally I was too exhausted to complain.

My dad had a maxim that he passed on to me, 'If you have one minute spare, sit down. If you have two minutes, lie down. If you have three minutes, go to sleep.'

In India, Charpoys were the habitat of the most evil bedbugs in the world. Standing the iron legs in tins of paraffin did not deter them, and once each week beds were stripped, the frames taken out on to the veranda and de-bugged with blow lamps. I was fortunate because for some unknown reason they did not find my blood to their liking. Maybe it was the alcohol in my bloodstream (or lack of it), but my opposite number in 'A' Section of the Machine Gun Troop, Piggy Lord, was virtually eaten alive. I was happier when the Regiment was on the move and we put the horses on Horse Lines and slept on the ground behind them using our saddles for a pillow. Mind you it was not policy to sleep too close behind them, even a shackled hoof could step on one's ear and horses were unpredictable when it came to lifting their tails. During the War I remembered my dad's advice many times and I certainly 'kipped' in some odd billets. Eight men in a bell-tent is not the height of luxury even if their feet are all directed towards the tent pole in the centre. Of course if the weather was fine you could always lift the flap and sleep with your head outside. And if you really want to get a crick in the back of your neck try sleeping in the Commander's seat of a Valentine tank or any other tank for that matter especially if it happens to be raining.

When the War ended and I was able to move into married quarters, bed became much more interesting for reasons which I do not intend to discuss. Also I did not have the responsibility for making the bed each morning.

It became even more luxurious when we were able to

41

dispense with the beds provided by the Quartermaster and buy our own.

Then, after I decided to leave the defence of the Realm to John and become a civilian and take Theresa Mona as my bed-mate, a new phase of luxury entered my life. Theresa Mona was difficult. I think it all started with the night of that first Easter when I put the gorgeous chocolate egg in her bed before I left for Tidworth and she stupidly switched on the electric blanket two hours before she retired for the night. Never will I forget her, 'I hate you! I hate you!' when she rang me up to tell me about her bed full of melted chocolate.

Strangely enough, both Kathleen and Theresa suffered from icy-cold feet and it seemed that only the heat from my healthy body could put warmth into them. Electric blankets, hot water-bottles and even thermal bed-socks did not work. Only the middle of my back was the answer. Then there was the Teas-Maid. Theresa Mona decided that early morning tea was my responsibility and I took charge of that inventive luxury. It was a bloody menace. I went to untold lengths each night to prepare it on its tray and carry it up to the bedside table and set the alarm – my side of the bed naturally. I would invariably set a wrong time on the alarm and it would go off in the middle of the night, or if I got the time right I would have omitted to put the tea into the pot and would pour out two cups of hot water. In the end I decided that it would be easier to get up each morning and go down to the kitchen and make it the old time-honoured way. Theresa never minded as long as she got her cups of tea. I did it for thirty years and still do out of force of habit.

Kathleen always liked reading in bed before she went off to sleep but because I was always the last to climb aboard, no sooner had I picked up my book then she would announce, 'Finished reading!' and switch off her bedside light. As she could not sleep with my light on my book never seemed to get read.

Theresa, on the other hand, would be asleep as soon as her head touched the pillow. But she had a habit of waking up in the middle of the night and deciding that she wanted to talk and discuss any little problem that she could think of. Invariably she would say as if she were dying of thirst, 'James, I would love a cup of tea, wouldn't you?'

I remember one night when she also felt hungry.

'James, I would love a piece of the lardy-cake I bought today.'

I got up to get her lardy-cake and as I left the room she added, 'And bring the Cribbage board. I'll play you once round the board for sixpence.'

Not only did she get her lardy-cake but she won and told me I owed her sixpence. She reminded me at breakfast.

And now that I am on my own, I would willingly get up in the night and get Maudie's lardy-cake or find Kathleen's bookmarker for her.

As one gets older sleep becomes more difficult, except at times when one should stay awake. I always remember Granny Page who would insist on me switching on the television so that she could watch the six o'clock News, and before Big Ben had completed his six bong bings she would be fast asleep.

Now the same thing happens to me. I sit down after my lunch, switch on to watch some cricket and wake up to find that I am watching *Children's Hour*. I meet other people who tell me that the television has the same soporific effect on them. The outcome is that I retire around the hour of 10 p.m. feeling quite sleepy, and then the old brain goes wandering off on its own drifting into a hundred and one different subjects and I find that I am wide awake.

I've tried counting sheep jumping over fences. That is useless. Someone once advised me to imagine that I was an old woollen sock lying limp and somnolent on the end of the bed. I have never yet been able to convert myself into an old sock.

Deep breathing and inhaling an excess of oxygen is recommended by the medical fraternity. That just makes me dizzy.

The only cure for insomnia is physical exercise. Flog the old body until it collapses into a coma. The trouble is that old age prevents worn out muscles from this treatment.

So, what is the answer? It's 3 a.m. and I still haven't dropped off. I switch on the bedside light, get up and go down and make a mug of tea. I put biscuits and cheese on a plate and stagger back to bed. I read a page of my book while I fill the bed with biscuit crumbs and drink the tea.

I switch off the light and in no time I'm in the Land of Nod.

But not for long it seems because I just start to get interested in an exciting dream and that black heathen of a cat jumps on the bed to tell me that he wants his breakfast. One day I'll find out who that blonde is!

Now it's time for my afternoon nap so this thesis on beds and sleep must come to an end.

I hope that you will find it instructive for when you have the same problem.

Sleep well my children,

Your P.O.G.

*   *   *

24 August 1992

Dear All,

Yesterday was August the twenty-third, Kathleen's birthday. She would have been seventy-eight. I went to eight o'clock Communion and said my prayers for the departed. The Vicar is having his annual holiday and his stand-in defeated me. He said the *Creed* even faster than I could. I had only got as far as 'suffered under Pontius Pilate' when I heard him say 'Amen'.

He beat me by a short head in the *Lord's Prayer* too and I thought no one could do that. In fact, I have never been to such a speedy service. I was back home before 8.30 a.m. eating toast and marmalade.

Betty and Jamie woke me up at 10.30 a.m. They came in for the usual Sunday morning Jamaican Coffee. I ate a frugal lunch and watched England lose the One-Day Test by three runs, and then the Three Day Event from Gatcombe Park. Lulu must have been furious because she does not like Pippa Nolan.

I ended the day with a good film that I had recorded on video for emergency when there was nothing else worth watching.

And so to bed. For some unaccountable reason Sam decided to join me around 1 a.m. He had just come in and was soaking wet. There is no peace for the wicked.

Today, believe it or not, today is the twenty-fourth. The weatherman on the early morning news assured me that a howling gale from America is imminent which did not surprise me. Very little good ever comes from America. So, assuming that for once they might be right, I decided to take my constitutional amble round the village while the sun was shining. I met Ann Christie who has just come out of hospital, so I had to stop and hear about her wounds. I saw a brand-new baby having a peep at the world for the first time and had a chat to Mr Sorsby at John O'Pease Cottage. He was at the top of a ladder giving an unruly clematis a haircut.

In the churchyard I had a brief word with Theresa Mona and then sat on the seat and allowed my mind to wander.

A card from Nicola this morning informed me that they were gorging themselves on cream teas in Ludlow. At least she and Kate were. Richard apparently is to join them tonight for a flog along Offa's Dyke.

Susan and Phillip should be somewhere near The Pyrenees by now while Katharine, I understand, is learning Italian with her boyfriend somewhere south of Rome and Joanna, so I am told, is in Guildford.

The Horse People at Tollard Park Equestrian Centre are, so I was told last night on the phone, having a 'Fun Day'. How anyone can have a 'Fun Day' with those long-faced, pin-brained, four-legged beasts is beyond me.

John and Taffy, I imagine, are in Cornwall living on a diet of prawns and bass. Emma, the last I heard, is somewhere walking between Mexico and Cape Horn.

I imagine that at this time of the year Hermione and Roger will be eating frogs' legs and snails and washing them down with local wines somewhere in France.

Michael and Mary are probably the only ones working, although they do sometimes disappear into the land of shamrocks and blarney stones.

And so you see I enjoy browsing and imagining what you are

up to. I went into the church and asked the Boss to keep an eye on you all.

Staggering down School Lane on my way home, I met Alan Pentycross and we agreed that the world was in a degenerate and immoral mess from the Royal Family downwards.

I had a brief chat to Leslie Harrison who I had not seen for some time.

Her views on publishers are on a par with my own.

With my strength ebbing fast I reached No. 17, unlocked the door and just managed to pour myself a medicinal gin and tonic which I have sipped while writing this 'A day in the life of P.O.G.' and now I shall need a reviving potion.

I wonder how far wrong my imagination has taken me?

I must also think about some solid nourishment. Man cannot live on gin and tonics alone.

I trust you are all enjoying life,

Your nearly ancient P.O.G.

*　*　*

27 August 1992

Dear All,

I am disconsolated, discouraged, disenchanted, disgusted, disheartened, dismayed and every other 'dis'.

My England is going downhill faster than I can keep up with it. It seems that we are now reaching an all time low. Morally, financially, politically, religiously and any other way one can think of.

My day did not start well. My doorbell rang. Guess who it was? A well-dressed young man and a young woman. Jehovah's Witnesses! Before I could shut the door they had started to expound The Revelation of St John the Divine. For a brief moment I was defeated, but getting my breath back I decided to give them a theological lecture. The Archbishop himself could not have done better. In no time at all I had them speechless and hopping from one foot to the other. I dismissed them with an exhortation to walk up the hill to St Mary's Church and have a

46

chat to the Lord himself. I think they were glad to escape although I doubt that they took my advice. What strange people they are.

As I stated, my day did not start well. Those sort of visits upset me. The news and weather forecasts were not encouraging either, although as I do not intend to join the Bank Holiday rush to the seaside, the weather will not affect me. However, I did have visions of Richard, Nicola and Kate staggering along Offa's Dyke in a howling gale and not a pub within miles.

The news was just a depressing saga of civil war in Bosnia, starving children in Somaliland and racial riots in Germany. Not to mention Hurricane Andrew in Florida.

Here on this island of ours, the Prime Minister seems to spend his days seeking answers to everyone's problems except our own. If the permanent smile with which he greets the cameras is anything to go by he must be succeeding. Mr Lamont also smiles at the cameras and assures us that the pound is in good shape and that we have nothing to worry about. I am sceptical. My pounds seem to buy less as the weeks go by.

Morally, the nation is beset by horrifying pictures and stories of our younger Royals indulging in sexual cavortings. It is only to be expected when they allow the press and the media to allude to them as Fergie, Di or Randy Andy. Familiarity breeds contempt and I am one who believes that the old courtesies should be maintained. Even in our little village I hear people calling the Doctor by his Christian name and likewise the Vicar. To me they will always be the Doctor or the Rector in public.

Those that hold High Office should be beyond reproach.

Those members of the Government who cannot be trusted in their private lives are not fit to arrange the affairs of their fellow citizens. They should set an example to those they represent. I remember Mr MacMillan, when he was Prime Minister, resigning only because he had trusted a member of his cabinet. The man had lied to him and he felt that he was not fit to be Prime Minister if he could not make sound judgements of those that he elevated to High Office.

The young Royals have the future integrity of our country in their hands. They should be setting an example to our younger generation in this age of permissiveness. The gutter press are having a financial birthday.

The Age of Sex again. The female of the species seems to be more obsessed with sex than the male. Glancing through the pages of an up-market women's magazine the other day, I was amazed at the emphasis on the subject. The girls seem to be enjoying it. I give you a brief insight. My attention was first drawn to the Book Section:

> *There's the Rubber.* The Condom book for girls. A hilarious bedtime read for all those interested in safe sex and foreign parts.

They were giving away twenty free copies. Then I noticed an advertisement for Heinz Beans:

> 'Beans Meanz . . . Sex.' Sex and beans can mix.
> At least at Asda where subtly sexy black velvet briefs are offered along with the weekly groceries.

The journal had ten sets to give away.

I perused my way through pages of beautiful girls adorning their charms in 'inspiring undies' and came across a most enlightening article entitled, 'Are the beautiful better in bed?'

It left me thinking of Rudyard Kipling's poem, *The Ladies.*

> For the Colonel's Lady and Judy O'Grady
> are sisters under the skin.

I finally came to the 'H' Bomb. All about hormones:

> Do hormones make you happy, horny or even hairy?

My doctor called me in before I could read further. One can always get a good read in his waiting room.

But take heart you males, there is still hope. I quote Mr

Auberon Waugh in *The Daily Telegraph:*

> The Army is among the very few areas of our national life which has not succumbed to the general demoralisation attendant on the collapse of the bourgeois ascendancy.

Mr Waugh also goes on to say that we have an education system in tatters, and a younger generation largely corrupted by the Dole and Income Supplement option. I sincerely hope that he is making an overstatement. I am putting all my hopes on my grandchildren to rectify all the mistakes that I have made.

I read somewhere the other day that,

> Crime is rampant, morality is at rock bottom, bankruptcies are soaring, the Church is in a turmoil, and aggression is replacing good manners as the hallmark of the nation.

Help! I am getting the impression that Sodom and Gomorah were virtuous when compared with LA and the cities of the Western World. I shall not be surprised when one day walking in the main street of Farnham to see 'Pillars of salt' gracing the pavements.

So my children, I am putting all my hopes on you. You have a duty to protect and preserve our inheritance of family values.

It is up to you to set the example by trying your utmost to live as decently as possible according to God's laws and despite the often-disgusting behaviour of others.

I've said it before. It's all yours kids. No one listens to me. Even my trigger finger is so crippled with arthritis that I shall never achieve my ambition to be the oldest hit-man in the world.

I leave you with a proverb that I read somewhere not long ago.

If there be righteousness in the heart there will be

beauty in the character.
If there be beauty in the character there will be harmony in the home.
If there be harmony in the home there will be order in the nation
When there is order in each nation there will be peace in the world.

Keep your powder dry,
Again your P.O.G.

*   *   *

12 September 1992

Dear All,

I always know when it is autumn. My neighbours deluge me with blackberry and apple pies. The Virginia Creeper starts to don its autumn colours and the garden begins to look untidy. There is a nip in the air and the evenings begin to close in. Football begins to dominate television and the children are all back at school preparing for half-term.

The summer holidays are now memories with everyone recuperating after the annual safaris to France, Italy, the Costa Brava and Disney Land.

I indulge in a search of my favourite autumn fruits: fresh English chestnuts, walnuts and cob nuts. I get frustrated when I try to find ripe Victoria plums or English apples. They always pick them long before they are really ripe so seldom can I find a really juicy plum that will allow the kernel to fall out and the juice dribble down my chin. In fact English fruit is almost unattainable. Everything in the supermarket is imported from the remotest parts of the world. Not only fruit. Vegetables with labels telling me that they are produce from Egypt, Israel, South Africa, Majorca and seemingly anywhere but England. I even saw peas in the pod imported from the USA.

Life ain't what it used to be. Shopping is no longer a pleasure. Yesterday I decided that I would like a cod cutlet. I would

50

imagine that it was caught weeks ago somewhere around Iceland. I looked at lobster and asked the price; £7 a pound!

Sea bass £3 a pound! Unbelievable but true. My days of lobster salads are now things of the past and I shall never again taste sea bass unless John catches me one.

I feel guilty everytime I buy food for Sam. I look at the vast array of pet foods. Whiskers, Arthur, Kattomeat, Pedigree Chum, Pal, Go-Cat, Brekkies; a whole aisle devoted to dozens of different choice dishes for dogs and cats. I think that what we lavish on our pets would feed the starving Somali people for a year and still leave some over for the rest of the Third World.

I'm getting morbid again. For all that I like the autumn. My mind starts drifting into quiet thoughts of Christmas. Yesterday I even bought two 1993 calendars! Dodo Diaries. I also bought a pot of marmalade. It stated on the label that it was 'A Full Half Pound'! Is there an 'over-full' or an 'under-full' half pound? Surely a half pound is a half pound. Neither over nor under. It reminds me of when I ask someone how far it is to somewhere and they tell me that is it just a 'short mile'!

I don't know why I'm writing all this rubbish. My mind wanders from one place to the next.

Susan is back from The Pyrenees loaded with duty-free vino and a healthy suntan. Phillip looks exhausted, pale and financially embarrassed. I boxed his answerphone for him by pressing the record button after a power cut so instead of a waiting list of potential customers, all he got was Betty and I discussing the feeding of Wellington the cat.

Richard and Nicola returned safely from their delve into the past, walking Offa's Dyke. A nasty dangerous place. The Welsh are still apt to forage over the border and steal the cattle and rape the women.

The Horse People at Tollard Royal are beset with the plague. A vicious virus that has laid half the work force at death's door. I always told them that those long-faced, four-legged beasts only spelt trouble.

I have no news of the rest of the tribe. John, I assume, is still guarding what is left of the Empire and making plans for the invasion of Bosnia.

No news from Hermione or Michael but no news can only be good news.

The Prime Minister is still all smiles assuring me that inflation is at its lowest ever level and that the Pound Sterling is as safe as the Bank of England. I am not altogether excited about either statement.

Lord (Doctor) Owen has been elevated to the role of 'Peace Negotiator'. If he is as successful in that sphere as he was in the medical profession and in his career in politics, the troubles in Yugoslavia will probably develop into World War Three. It seems that a bogged-up job in government is the surest way to the ranks of the peerage. David Steele only got a Sir. Mind you he's still got a nice cushy little job in Brussels. I wonder what Paddy Ashdown has in mind for himself? Perhaps he would be happy with a new secretary.

Mr Mellor still thrives on the publicity from his interesting sexual forays. I think even his choice of partner for his fun and games is open for criticism. A sad skinny-looking female in my view.

Now we are going to send the army out to protect the rations. Good old Tommy Atkins to the rescue once more. All the mums and dads will be up in arms if any of them get shot at.

What else has been brought to my notice during the past few weeks? Oh Yes! The Born Again Christians!

I am not altogether sure that what I have heard about this new adventure into the realm of religion is accurate, but I am given to understand that they now have priority with our Maker. They have a 'hot-line' to Heaven and their prayers get immediate attention. God, I understand, gave one young lady last week an order to go to Italy for reasons known only to Him. There must be something in it because although she had no visible means of support, she was apparently transported to Heathrow where I believe a ticket was waiting for her, and to the best of my knowledge she is now a guest of the Italians. Thomas Cook and Lunn Poly will be put out of business if they are not careful.

I believe that these 'Born Again Christians' only have to get on their knees and voice their requests to get immediate satisfaction. Betty is contemplating joining and asking for her poll tax to be paid.

There must be something in it because it seems that the line is invariably engaged when I try to get a little whisper in. I shall have to find out more about it.

I shall go to early morning Communion tomorrow and perhaps I'll be able to get through before they are all up.

It is probably very wrong of me to belittle them. At least they are firm in their beliefs even if I think they are somewhat misguided. Who am I to criticise when even some of my own kith and kin either do not believe in anything or do not practise what they profess to believe in.

I shall ask for forgiveness tomorrow and pray for you lot as well.

Now I shall stop this drivel and go for my constitutional amble around the village before it starts to rain again.

I will write again when I have something really good to bleat about.

As always,

Your exhausted P.O.G.

*   *   *

14 September 1992

My Dear Children,

I know that you will most likely disagree with me and say that I am living in a world of the past, but I am certainly worried about the world of the future, especially this beloved country of ours.

Perhaps I am partly to blame, being one of those who thirty years ago sought the easy life, and perhaps we were the nation that 'never had it so good', but today events have caught up with us and I find that our society is not as safe, happy and permanent as I once thought.

This England of the 1990s, with its violence and crime, is far from being Mr Major's 'nation at ease with itself'.

Ringing in our ears is not the sound of English church bells

53

and the laughter of children, but the screaming of protest marchers, baying for the blood of the society that they revile. A terrible realisation has now dawned on me that the England that I trusted, took for granted and loved, is slowly slipping away, perhaps never to be recovered.

A prime example is the issue of Europe. You must realise that the 'ever-closer union' to which we are being committed will eventually mean the effective end of the British Monarchy? You must realise that the leading federalists are by nature anti-Monarchist. And that when Britain becomes a Europrovince, our well-loved symbols such as the Union Jack, the Royal Standard and even the Queen's own head on the pound coin will be replaced by the rootless, artificial symbols of the new Eurostate. Our Queen and the ancient Parliament which gives her allegiance will be completely subordinate to the faceless power-structure of the European Community, and eventually, when we are fully governed from the high-tech office blocks in Brussels, Crown and State will have disappeared altogether. The old offices of Prime Minister and Chancellor, and the centuries-old Monarchy itself, will be de-commissioned by our bureaucratic masters, and as a final act of triumph they will lower the Union Jack and hoist the yellow-starred flag of Europe above Buckingham Palace and Westminster.

All across Britain, and what remains of the Anglo-Saxon world overseas, ordinary people like me are praying that this appalling prospect never becomes a reality. Indeed, in France, Spain and Germany loyal citizens of those states are praying also that they will escape what the writer Paul Johnson has described as 'death by a thousand Brussels cuts'.

You must already know that the little men – the Politicians – are poised to sell our country out. This sad fact we have bitterly, but philosophically, come to accept. In truth, we didn't expect much from them anyway, so we were not surprised, just disappointed.

Perhaps Her Majesty the Queen will express disapproval as the ship of state is steered into the dark waters of European Federalism. As our nation begins it descent into the abyss we should look to her for help. Our nation faces the greatest threat that it has ever faced since 1940 and we must be prepared to fight it. To make a fight of it, we need to be inspired.

You my children, must be prepared to defend our ancient island birthright, our national heritage and the Monarchy that we all treasure so much.

Most of what I have said I have quoted from writings of better educated men than me but it is very true.

Don't let them give our Britain away. I wish that I could find a wonderful article that I read recently entitled 'Don't Let Europe Rule Britannia'. If I can locate it I shall certainly make an effort to send it on.

Anyway the title speaks for itself and for me.

All my love,

Your optimistic P.O.G.

*   *   *

4 October

Dear All,

September has disappeared and October has arrived with a cold north-east wind. September seemed to fly by in a spate of tidying up the garden, mostly done by Betty, and visits from all and sundry. The garden is not yet completely tucked-up for the winter and there are still bulbs to be planted.

The first visitors were Pauline and Chloe. We enjoyed a pleasant visit to the Country Market and lunched in the new eating-house. Angela dashed in one afternoon. I forget the day. She had been to London Airport to send Justin off to Indonesia and all stations east. She just had time for a cup of tea and a chat before dashing off to do some more 'mucking-out'.

Next was Georgia. A fleeting visit to say goodbye before she started her adventures with Sir Walter Raleigh. She is now somewhere in Chile doing good works and playing her panpipes to the Indians.

There was also one weekend and for the life of me I can't remember which, when Susan and Phillip took a weekend in France and I fed Welly their cat for them. I think that they only went to stock up with more duty-free plonk.

My doorbell rang one afternoon waking me from my 'deep dream of peace'. It was Hermione. She was returning from Cambridge where she had deposited her No. 1 son to continue his academic studies at Kings. She too could only spare a couple of hours and a quick drive to see Susan in the Bank at Four Marks.

Lastly, although I could be wrong because I vaguely remember Richard and Knickers looking in, Michael and Mary arrived exhausted after a day in London. They stayed the night and we finalised their visit with lunch at the Anchor.

And now I am getting my breath back and able to catch up with all the news and chaos that is currently taking place in this troubled world.

I could not help thinking this morning as I heard the Vicar intoning the prayers, '. . . and specially thy servant *Elizabeth* our Queen; that under her we may be godly and quietly governed,' and I wondered if the congregation listened to the politicians all shouting at one another during *Westminster Live.* Similarly with '. . . that they may truly and indifferently administer justice, to the punishment of wickedness and vice.' I wondered whether Mr Mellor or Cecil Parkinson felt any pangs of conscience. I nearly forgot Paddy Ashdown.

Fortunately, with so many visitors I missed most of the shouting and tub-thumping by the Opposition Party in Blackpool, but what little I did hear did not fill me with any great feelings of relief. I wonder why they sing the *Red Flag* and not the National Anthem at the termination of their conference. Actually it seems to me to be a shouting match rather than an intelligent week of conferring.

This week it is the turn of the Government to endeavour to justify all their mistakes.

At least I did humbly beseech Our Lord to comfort and succour all them, in this transitory life that are in trouble, sorrow, need, sickness and any other adversity.

I can only hope that He heard me. I get a mental picture of a massive Heavenly Office with a staff of thousands sitting at desks tapping our prayers into computers and passing them on to Head Office for action. Rather on the lines of a gigantic earthly 'phone-in'.

Reply paid prayers! I hope that the Heavenly Head Office is more efficient than the publishers that I write to. SAEs don't mean a thing to them.

And now from downstairs I smell the scent of my stew wafting upwards. It is probably boiling over.

I shall stop this drivel and go down with the hope that all is well and that October proves as pleasant as September. It will go almost as quickly no doubt. Not quite because it is one day longer.

Happy Days. Love to you all.

Your P.O.G.

* * *

17 October 1992

My Dear Georgia,

What a wonderful surprise. A letter from Chile. I had no idea that it would be possible. I thought that one had to send letters by natives carrying the missive in a cleft stick. I wonder if the service from our Royal Mail will be as efficient. I shall be most surprised if this ever reaches you.

I am delighted that Sir Walter is living up to your expectations but I must honestly admit that I am glad it is you and not me. It takes my mind back to Afghanistan. The only difference, as far as I can see, is that we had no radio and had to communicate via heliograph and the natives took two months to deliver a letter to England in their cleft sticks. It was quite a run for them. I also remember the violent changes in the temperature. During the day it would be about 120 degrees in the shade and ten below after sunset. That is where they coined the phrase 'the sands of the desert grow cold'.

But joking apart, I am delighted that you are enjoying the adventure and I know that you will achieve wonders.

Life in good old Bentley, as you call it, wanders on at its own leisurely pace. We are currently into the bulb-planting/leaf-sweeping-up time of the year. Betty has been slaving in both our gardens tucking them up for the winter while I give expert advice from the lounge window. Sam now has a choice of lavatories in the newly-dug flower beds. He is still enjoying his mouse followed by the cream-off-the-milk diet.

Last Sunday was Harvest Festival and we ploughed the fields and scattered in good voice. Actually I was rather remiss. I failed to wake up in time and had to leave the 'Thanks be to God' to Betty. I don't know what I would do without her. I have even got her doing my praying for me now.

I have not seen nor heard of your devoted parents for some weeks. I understand that pater has been bitten by the golf bug and now spends his leisure hours trying to improve his swing. I think that he is a little afraid that you might beat him when you return to this currently unhappy island. We are in the doldrums. Recession, pit closures, unemployment reaching an unprecedented high, and beer £16 a gallon. Actually the sun is shining today and I am sipping a medicinal gin and tonic as I write. The 'Masticate Treaty', not the right word but it will suffice, is out of my sphere of influence although I am very, very anti being rechristened a Euroman. I want to remain English.

While waiting for publishers to make their minds up about my masterpiece I have started another one, the title of which is 'The Inside Bit' although I doubt that it will mean much to you. I hope to have it completed before your return and then I shall look forward to your expert criticism.

I had a postcard from Emma yesterday. She too is in Chile but I could not decipher the location. If you see her give her my love. I think she is somewhere near the Argentine border.

Your Uncle Michael and Aunt Mary descended on me last weekend craving beds. They seem in good spirits and Michael made a good job of depleting my wine cellar. Other than that I have no news. The Horse People are still mucking out and I believe David and Angela have moved into their new home. Susan has acquired another puppy which, although I have not yet seen it has been named Co-Co.

I wish I had something interesting to write about but I can only say thank you for your so interesting description of your travels. I shall look forward to future news.

58

Now I shall see if the Royal Mail has a means of getting this to you.

Look after yourself and take care.

All my love,

Your increasingly ancient P.O.G.

*   *   *

1 November 1992

My Dear Children,

The last few days of October were memorable.

Firstly Angela arrived on Wednesday evening in time for dinner, and we sat until midnight dwelling in the past and discussing the trials and tribulations of Tollard Park Equestrian Centre.

We enjoyed a leisurely meal encouraged by an extremely nice claret.

On Thursday we shopped at the Country Market, browsed over the incredible Christmas display at Forest Lodge and finished with a hilarious lunch at the Anchor Inn at Lower Froyle to which we also invited Betty. Angela left for her return journey in the late evening back to the mucking-out and care of fifty or more horses. I had an early night to prepare for the rigours of Friday the thirtieth.

My first task on rising was to remove my dinner jacket from the wardrobe, shake out all the moths and hang it out to air and dispense the odour of mothballs. John was to pick me up at 4 p.m. and drive me to the last Officers' Mess Dinner in the Regiment.

He arrived just a little too early and was in time to tie the shoe lace of my right shoe. It persists in remaining out of my reach. Having secured me safely in the passenger seat and belted me up, I navigated him by short cut to the M3. Then it was up to him. He had said that he wished to leave early to avoid the rush hour traffic. To me it was chaos and when he informed me that we were on the M25 it was just a world gone mad. We somewhere or other left the M25 and I saw signs reading M11. It was no different from the other Ms. We seemed to be following thousands of rear lights stretching as far as the eye could see with thousands of head lights attacking us on our right front. A new moon hanging in the sky on our right would suddenly appear on our left. John seemed to know exactly where he was going while I just crossed my fingers.

'Just keep your eyes open for a sign to Saffron Walden, Dad,' he ordered. As without glasses I could only just see the sign-board, let alone read what it said, he was asking the impossible. However, he found it without my aid and we were then in a maze of dark country roads. Somehow he found Carver Barracks and was depositing me into the care of a young officer outside the mess while he parked the car. I thought what a splendid son I had produced.

We were early. I was able to lose myself in a world of nostalgia and wander round feasting my eyes on all the familiar oils, pictures and trophies that I had not seen for so many years. I sat awhile in the ante-room, lost in memories.

Then old friends and comrades began to drift in. It took me back into another age. They hadn't changed, just got a little older. Then as the gathering multiplied the cacophony of voices rose to a high point that defeated my electric ears. But it didn't matter that I could not hear what was being said. Just to be part of it all was enough.

We posed for a photograph in the huge gymnasium: nearly 200 officers, past and present. How that will ever come out I just cannot imagine. Then the dinner itself. A masterpiece of culinary organisation that can only be described as magnificent. The Regimental Band playing selections of old favourites. It was an occasion that none of us would ever forget. Then it was all over. John and I could not stay the night. He had a duty to perform at first light back at Tidworth. He drove me to my home, 180 miles, and saw me safely in before he continued his journey.

But he did return before lunch on Saturday and we were able to hie to the Anchor Inn where John was able to indulge in a pint or two of well-earned Hardy Country Ale. He had not been able to drink more than an odd glass of wine at the dinner. But we enjoyed a get together on our own that we are seldom able to manage.

But all good things must end. John had to return to his duties and the bosom of his family.

It was after he had left and I was sitting quietly on my own that a wave of sadness pervaded my being. My mind savoured the pleasure of the previous evening and then it struck me that it was the end of an era. Never again would we get together for an officers' dinner of the 16th/5th The Queen's Royal Lancers. The little men – the Politicians, with a stroke of a pen were closing the book on another page of British history. The Regiment that had played its part over centuries of keeping England safe and secure was to be no more. They were to be merged with the 17th/21st who would also lose their identity. They would be feeling the same sense of frustration. The Charge of the Light Brigade and The Battle of Aliwal would be shared in their memories.

I could not help the sense of tragedy that I felt. In a way it was the same that assailed me when my Kathleen was killed that day on the road to Osnabruck as we were on our way to the Regiment. It was like the closing of a book. The End.

And yet, it was the Regiment that picked me up and put me on my feet. The loyalty and comradeship that gave me strength to carry on. And so I know that the spirit of two great Cavalry Regiments will be merged and be ready when they are needed. The words from Kipling's *If* spring to my mind:

> If you can make one heap of all your winnings
> And risk it all on one turn of pitch and toss,
> And lose, and start again at your beginnings
> And never breathe a word about your loss;
> If you can force your heart and nerve and sinew
> To serve your turn long after they are gone,
> And so hold on when there is nothing in you
> Except the Will which says to them: 'Hold On!'

And now it is November. I am back here with Samson my cat and my thoughts.

61

Thomas Hood must have been feeling much the same as he wrote:

No sun – no moon!
No morn – no noon!
No dawn – no dusk – no proper time of day.
November!

I had better get out and rake up some leaves. Press on regardless James.

Perhaps a gin and tonic would cheer me up.

Love to you all,

Your rather sad P.O.G.

* * *

25 November 1992

Dear All,

We had a day called 'Black Wednesday' when something went wrong with the country's finances and now we have had Black November.

It started with Guy Fawkes Day which, in the days of my youth, used to be celebrated on November the fifth.

Now it starts on the fourth and continues up until the eighth.

Actually in the village 'Bonfire Night' was on the sixth. All those evenings were dry and fine and the pyrotechnics on the sixth were quite spectacular. I watched them from the bedroom window. Sam did not approve. He spent every evening on the above dates beneath the bed with his paws over his ears.

It started to rain on the ninth, and apart from a few isolated moments, the weather has been foul ever since reaching a peak of horridness today. Fortunately I need only venture forth during the isolated moments.

Then when all the crackers and rockets were expended the Canterbury Synod had their vote on the Ordination of Women. The women won. They have their feet under the Lord's table at

62

last. The last male fortress has been breached. As I have said before God must take some, if not all, of the blame on Himself. Had He not allowed the Eve woman to go scrumping in the Garden of Eden this battle of the sexes might never have started. The girls have been scrumping ever since. I can put my finger on very few occupations that are still a male monopoly. I have not yet noticed a female refuse collector and, to date, I don't think we have a female judge although I did hear that lady barristers are complaining of sex discrimination. Keep trying girls. You'll make it. I visualise a world completely dominated by woman-power before the end of the century. If you walk past Boadicea's statue you will probably see the smile on her face. There is a faint ray of hope. We males will always be in demand if there is ever a mouse in the kitchen or a spider in the bath. So keep your pecker up chaps. In more ways than one, I might add!

On top of all that Windsor Castle is in flames. What a dreadful year it has been for Her Majesty. I for one can only feel utterly sorry for her. To have it happen after all the family problems that she has suffered is like getting another slap in the face. And now we have the Mr Smith, Mr Cook MP and the rest on the Opposition benches howling about who is to pay for the restoration. Well it gives them the opportunity to shout a little louder and expel a lot more hot air.

Our Prime Minister is still cantering around Europe trying to put things right. He must have shaken hands and been photographed with every politician the other side of the Channel. And this side. I wonder why Colegate have not snapped him up as an advert for their toothpaste. Perhaps they have.

I am intrigued also by a number of other things that I am confronted with daily. I had no idea until these past few months that so many people earned their living as 'analysts'. Not a day goes by without an analyst appearing on our television screens. There are analysts for every conceivable subject I can think of, and many that I can't. I wonder who pays their salaries.

Again it seems that each day I meet a new lord. Lord Parkinson, Lord Tebbitt, Lord Owen, Lord Archer, Lord St John, Lord Lawson. I must have missed the New Year's Honours List. I dread to think what Mr Kinnock will get. An Earldom maybe, although I see that the BBC has asked him to take over from Jimmy Young. I think a disc jockey should be right up his street.

And here I am without even an OBE or even a mention. Mind you my late CO assured me that OBE stood for 'Other Bugger's Efforts' so that lets me out. Nobody makes any effort to help me except old Betty and besides that I don't know any buggers.

It's a funny old world now. A short while ago the word on everybody's lips was inflation. Now it has changed to redundancy. Inflation I am told is at its lowest level which surprises me because the price of everything is going up. I do wish one of you would come and give me some instruction on modern finance. I hear and read about millions and billions but I can still only think in terms of pounds, shillings and pence.

And now Christmas is just around the corner.

In fact it has been in Farnham since the beginning of October. My goose is not getting any fatter. I don't like goose anyway.

I must stop all this nonsense. November has not been the best of months for anyone as far as I can make out.

I understand that down at Tollard Park they are building an ark so you know where to go to if the rain keeps up.

So for now,

Love in rum and dry gingers,

Your thirsty P.O.G.

* * *

16 December 1992

My Dear Children,

The festival of Christmas is just a few days hence. Seventy-nine years have disappeared into the past and I am feeling older. But then I am older than I was last year.

Somehow I have lost my enthusiasm. They tell me that it is because Christmas is now so commercialised but it isn't that. I think that for the first time I have come to realise that I have no one to share the preparations with except Sam and he merely objects to anything that upsets his routine. It used to be fun going out to buy presents with Theresa Mona and choosing gifts that would be pleasing and original. Now I seem to have lost the urge. You have all grown up and have everything. So I just remember Christmases past.

From a soldier's Christmas on the Afghan border, Egypt, North Africa, France, Belgium, Germany, the Islands and dear old Blighty.

I remember some more than others. The Christmas of the 'Flaming Pudding' in Cyrenacia when James used methylated spirits instead of brandy to produce the desired effect.

The Christmas when Richard, John and Michael consumed a ten-pound York ham, a huge jar of pickled onions and a whole barrel of beer for their breakfasts alone. That was before they took unto themselves wives and all the problems that went with them.

The Christmas of the false eyelashes in Alderney when Theresa put them on upside down. That was before Susan and Hermione got themselves involved with the male sex.

The Christmas of the carol singers when the Rector gradually saw his choir being encouraged to imbibe more rum punch and more mince pies than was conducive to *Away in a Manger*, and when Reverend Peter Shaw blessed the house of Mr Paul Crombie and all who sailed in her.

The Christmas of the snow when the tribe of Richard and Nicola ruined all Granny's tea trays on the toboggan run.

I could go on. Each Christmas with a special memory. Now they don't seem the same. It is an effort. Everyone is in such a rush. No one has time to think about the real reason behind it all.

I remember the Christmas when little Katharine looked at my birthday calendar and saw 'Jesus' on the twenty-fifth. She went into fits of laughter and it was ages before we could establish the cause of her merriment. She wondered how Grandad James was going to send Him a birthday card!

But that really is what it is all about. It is a birthday party for the most famous baby of all time. I sometimes think that the beauty of it all is lost in a great hurly-burly of rushing from party to party exuding alcoholic goodwill on all and sundry.

The simple family Christmas of my childhood had much more meaning. But one can't go back.

I have got to be indoctrinated with ugly television puppets performing a modern version of Dickens' *Christmas Carol* and probably *Crocodile Dundee* and a load of American 'Blood and Thunder'. I am told that it is progress.

So I am sad.

I am an old grumble.

Forgive me.

I hope with all my heart that you will all have a happy time in your homes and please do give a little thought to the reason behind it all.

Now I will just wish you all a Merry Christmas and also a very Prosperous 1993.

I shall hang my stocking up at Tollard Royal.

My love to you all,

Your ancient Grumble P.O.G.

* * *

31 December 1992

My Dear Tribe,

In thirteen hours and ten minutes I shall have made it. Old Father Time will be able to put away his scythe until 1993. Mind you, there were odd moments during the past twelve months when I thought that I would not make it so if I can make the next few hours, success will be mine.

Then all you will have to do is keep your fingers crossed for a further year. That is of course if you wish me to remain in this lovely old world.

Christmas, as it usually does, came and went in a welter of presents, wrapping paper, rum punches and mince pies, cards from all over the world, carolling and a few moments wondering what it was all about. Regrettably, I rather feel that singing 'Happy Birthday Dear Jesus' is generally lost in the mad rush.

I spent a very happy few days with the Horse People at Tollard Royal. Christmas Day was spent undoing presents, toasting absent friends and eating. I had a long lie-in at the commencement while the horses were being watered and fed.

I will here take the opportunity of thanking you for the mass of gifts that you sent me. If I attempt to write individual thank-you letters I shall still be doing it this time next year. So, 'Thanks' one and all.

Boxing Day I spent at the cottage of Grandaughter Katie, and Pee (the Border Collie), Rosie, Harriet, Hector, Porter (the Jack Russells), Debussy and Monsieur Jaque (the cats), plus of course, David, Angela, Lulu and Dereck.

Twilight Boy (the horse; alias 'Tarry'), came to the back door to wish me Seasons Greetings and eat an apple. Again the day was spent feasting, drinking and playing games.

I was given two days in which to recover before Angela returned me to the safety of No. 17 Eggars Field.

Now here I am on the last day of the year taking a deep breath in preparation for 1993. I wonder what it will bring.

My 'Horrorscope' is not encouraging. Apparently I must pay particular attention to the conservation of finance. Healthwise, I am advised to avoid the medical profession and just continue with the occasional medicinal tot of rum. I am to avoid the female sex (especially those who wish to force germ-ridden kisses on me), say my prayers and trust the Lord.

Now I shall go and pour my medicinal rum punch, prepare my last lunch of 1992 and get ready to meet the problems of 1993.

I trust and hope that it will be a wonderful year for you all.

Keep smiling and remember K.K.K. (Kool, Kalm and Kollected) at all times.

God Bless and Love from your,
Optimistic P.O.G.

* * *

THE LETTERS OF P.O.G
1993

My Dear Children,

Two weeks of this New Year have already flown by and I have started it in a welter of pessimistic lethargy.

Why?

Probably because of the weather which has virtually kept me housebound. This morning has been the first day that I have managed my daily walk around the village and even that was marred by a freezing, sleety shower as I reached the church. I took refuge within and had a chat to the Lord until it had passed over. I think He was pleased to see me.

If my lethargy is not caused by the weather it may well be that I have been trying to assess my achievements of 1992 and found them sadly lacking. I had nine rejections from publishers, plus two from literary agents. I am fast becoming the most rejected writer in the world. I did complete the first saga of the adventures of Charles Henry Simpkins and the Reverend Tobias Jug but have not yet had the courage to submit them. In fact I also started the second adventures of my two heroes. Twenty-six letters of P.O.G. remain hidden in the file plus one or two military oddments which must be kept out of sight as they are unfit for human consumption.

So my literary efforts were a waste of time except that perhaps they kept my feeble brain from completely stagnating.

One thing that did please me was the fact that after many years, I located and made contact with my dear old friend Ken Peet. That was a masterpiece of detection worthy of Inspector Morse. I did also make the supreme effort and embark on my nostalgic journey to Castlemartin via Crocketts and Ross-on-Wye. Those two weeks were the highlight of my year.

So reflecting back, I did very little to make the world a better place.

I have also not made any New Year resolutions other than to try to mend all those that I broke last year.

The third reason for my despondency can be put down to the state of the world as presented to me by the various Media; Wars and genocide in Yugoslavia; starvation in the Third World;

chaos and mayhem in the Middle East between the Jews and Palestinians; Sadam Hussein still stirring it up in Iraq; oil pollution on the high seas; the Recession at home; unemployment rife; the Church in the war of women priests; muggings, murder and violence reported daily; the Royal Family in the centre of scandal and divorces; the destruction of our armed forces by the Politicians.

I could go on and on and find little but gloom.

Is it any wonder that I am in a state of pessimistic lethargy?

I know what I shall do. I shall retire downstairs, pour myself a rum punch, eat some shepherd's pie and then perhaps I shall be able to return to this machine in a happier frame of mind.

I shall do just that.

The rum helped but the shepherd's pie was not really exciting. Probably because I watched the one o'clock news while I ate it. The newsreaders seem to gloat as they disclose the latest selection of mayhem. They have reached the peak of efficiency where they can make even the reporting of a cricket match a saga of depression.

So again I reflect on my achievements. I have done 'Sweet Fanny Adams'. That is not quite true because I have discovered where that phrase originated.

The town of Alton in 1878. A little girl, seven years old, was murdered in the hop fields. The murderer cut her up into small pieces and scattered her remains over a large area of the hop fields so that Sweet Fanny Adams was never found to be buried. The little girl's name was Fanny Adams. The little that was found was buried in the parish churchyard and the memorial stone still stands there. The murderer was hanged.

Strange world.

Perhaps 1993 will see an improvement. Remain K.K.K. James, and press on regardless.

No more for now,

Your temporarily pessimistic P.O.G.

* * *

22 January 1993

My Dear Six,
My horoscope for the month of January reads:

LEO 24th July-23rd August
Slow down, recharge your batteries and analyse the
aims and ambitions that will be your driving force in
1993. Leo is associated with creativity and, although
you may not have the energy and vitality of Aries, you
have all the necessary shades and facets that are
gleaned from life's real experiences. What really
matters is the inspiration and new insight you will
gain at the time of the new moon on 22 January.

There. It is now the twenty-second, my batteries have been
recharged and I trust will remain so, although I fear that they
were very flat at the beginning of the month. I have a suspicion
that I need new ones.

I have not noticed any inspiration and new insight exuding
from my brain. Perhaps it will be apparent tomorrow
morning.

A new president has been installed in the USA and is already
facing his first crisis. President Bill Clinton will need all his
musical talent to survive. I personally think that he would have
been better employed playing his saxophone in Harlem.

Mr Major and the Right Honourable Leader of the Opposition
are, it would seem from *Westminster Live,* spending most of their
days shouting at each other from across the floor of the House.
Unemployment has reached Gargantuan proportions; pit
closures, or the threat thereof, are resurrecting Mr Arthur
Scargill; British Rail is in a mess, and it is suggested that
privatisation will lift it to new heights of efficiency which is a
very debatable point. The News this morning was expounding a
surge of racism and the birth of Fascism with hordes of militant
young men shouting in a similar style to their counterparts in
Germany raising their fists in angry Nazi-like gestures. The
Health Service is struggling to cope with the great influx of 'Sick,

73

Lame and Lazy'. I coin that phrase from my military days. Daily 'Sick Parade' was always preceded by a trumpet call so named.

The Press are up in arms about restrictions and laws of privacy being enforced on them. The Royal Family have got themselves into what can only be termed 'a bloody mess' of divorce and sexual scandals.

The weather is foul and north of the border the Scots are busy bailing out after the worst floods for decades.

World news is even worse. Organised rape is making headlines from Yugoslavia. Sadam Hussein is still strutting about with his Colt 45 on his hip vowing vengeance on the West, and the American Air Force is desperately trying to hit Iraqi missile sites. I believe that they have even been very close. They managed to drop one in El Rashid Street in Baghdad anyway.

There was one little glimmer of light from Somaliland with the smiling faces of the children at last getting some food. One can only hope that it will continue to improve.

And, believe it or not, I am told that the Recession is on the mend.

One friendly neighbour to whom I made that statement said, 'Bullshit!' which I thought was very rude.

Tell me. How am I going to get inspiration from that lot? I must ask Richard. *Christmas Crackers.* Certainly I have found no Insight or uplift from that, and Angela's gift of the *Oxford Book of Villains* is no help either.

Sam is my only hope together with the new moon tonight.

So, analysing my hopes and ambitions for 1993 has got off to a bad start.

Perhaps I had better seek help from Charles Henry Simpkins (deceased) and the Reverend Tobias Jug (also deceased).

Actually yesterday produced a very pleasant interlude. Georgia arrived just as Peter and Linda from next door were preparing to take me out to lunch, which resulted in a convivial feast at the Bull Inn.

I am a lucky bloke.

Pauline came on Wednesday to instruct me in the setting up of this processor, but although the resulting procedures are beneficial I have not the faintest idea of how she did it.

So 1993 has started now in a note of optimism. We shall continue the struggle with new vigour.

Three Cheers for the Red, White and Blue!

As Michael Haddock reports about the weather, 'The sun will shine one day with a bit of luck.'

Be good.

As ever,

P.O.G.

* * *

14 February

Dear All,

Here I am in the third week of February wondering what happened to January. I am still slowly emerging from a state of torpidity.

TORPID (of hibernating animals): dormant; numb; sluggish; apathetic; dull.

That's what my dictionary says. And it's true. To date I have only ventured forth into the New Year about five times, like the squirrel, just to gather a few nuts.

This morning I have, only with a great effort of will, been to early Communion to put a good word in for all of you who are too busy or too lazy to say your own prayers. The theme today was 'The sower going forth to sow'. A lot of his seed is falling on stony ground in this modern world of ours.

It is also St Valentine's Day. I only had one card and that was from one of my nine-year-old fans. I am not loved.

The prospect does not seem encouraging.

This first two weeks of the month were a little sad. I lost my neighbours. Peter and Linda could no longer afford to live in this much sought-after village. They have moved north to

75

Grantham where, I am led to believe, living is less expensive. Just when one gets to know and like people something always happens to bring one down to earth.

We did give them a splendid farewell dinner but it is not until the actual parting arrives and they have gone that the void is really felt. I shall miss them both very much.

Pauline came to see me on Thursday with Chloe. She cheered me up. She also brought the final draft of 'The Inside Bit'. Now all I have to do is find a publisher. Keep your fingers crossed and I may be lucky this time. She also drove me to the new Tesco in Aldershot. My first introduction to a 'superstore'. I was terrified. Never in the history of human conflict have I ever seen so much food displayed in one place.

It was a bewildering mass of humans (I think they were humans), all pushing great trolleys piled high with every conceivable edible product from all over the world. Not only food either. I noticed vast areas where medications were displayed under great signs stating 'Medical Health and Beauty Care'.

Tesco is not for James.

I persuaded Pauline to drive me to the Hen and Chickens so that I might be revived with a pint of medicinal beer. I survived.

Bentley is currently experiencing a wave of pilfering. They turned over old Mrs Silver's house and stole her few pennies. They even turned her mattress to see if she hoarded her savings there. She fortunately did not. It makes one wonder what our country is coming to when they want to rob a ninety-five-year-old lady. Someone also pinched the charity boxes from the shelf in the Post Office and believe it or not, a lamppost in the church carpark was dug up and removed. I think that we shall soon have to start putting down some poisoned bait. They put down Warfbait for rats don't they?

From the News I gather that the rest of the world is still in a turmoil. Inflation is down to 1.7% whatever that means. I read that milk is 33p a pint everywhere except Bentley, where it is 38p. Beer is now nearly £20 a gallon. The teachers are considering industrial action because of a meagre pay-rise being offered. Redundancy is more rife than ever and the politicians are squabbling like a load of petulant kids.

The newspapers and television in honour of St Valentine have devoted much space and hours of viewing to the subject of sex. The *Radio Times* displayed a special love number cover and devoted the whole weekend to the subject.

Friday: *Get a Grip on Sex* – a light-hearted video guide to sex with Mariella Frostrup; *Carnal Knowledge* – a sex quiz show; *Dream Doll* – animation about a man with an inflatable doll.

And that is only a sample.

Saturday: A Night of Love. Live from the Windmill Theatre, a Kissathon; a demonstration of condom art; *The Naked Chat Show*; *Sacred Sex*; animation about a couple's love life; and Margi Clarke's opinions of sex.

Sunday: (Continuing three days to celebrate St Valentine's Day,) *A Love Talk Special*; *Looking for Love* – poor Eric Meyer, he couldn't have a proper relationship because he found it difficult to relate to women.

Monday: *A Secret World of Sex*; *Unmarried Mums and their Problems*; *The Good Sex Guide* – Margi Clarke again entering the minefield of sexual etiquette, 'What are the worst crimes you commit between the sheets?'

Will 'Love Week' become a yearly event?

Marathon love-making contests; Effathons; Get in the *Guinness Book of Records*. A vast new sport. They will probably introduce first, second and third divisions like football, all competing for 'The Gold Condom', 'Benson and Hedges World Championship'. I ought to become a promoter or a trainer. I would probably make a fortune. It might be a good idea to start an oyster farm. I must think about it.

'Red Nose Week' is upon us again. I had the pamphlet delivered yesterday with a new array of ways to use the Red Nose to raise more and more money for charity.

I wonder what Easter will bring. The Easter eggs and hot cross buns are already on sale.

Perhaps the Archbishop of Canterbury will come up with something really exciting.

I must stop.

Who's for bed? Sam has already turned in so I had better wend my way to the old Charpoy.

I wonder if I can find my copy of the Kama Sutra? I told you a long time ago that we were now in the age of sex.

Goodnight all. Perhaps that luscious blonde will come back tonight!

Sweet dreams,

Your past-it, old P.O.G.

* * *

7 March 1993

Dear All,

The 'Nones of March'. It's the Ides that one has to beware of. That's the fifteenth, and you know what happened to Julius Caesar? You see, more useless information.

February has gone into history. It went out with a freezing-cold tail which has been with us right up until today.

I nearly went out and did some gardening but allowed myself to be lured before the television to watch England defeat Scotland at Twickenham. A change, to say the least, after the debacle of our cricketers in India.

Now I can start looking forward to the spring. Only two weeks of winter left, then perhaps I shall have something interseting to write about. What have I done since I wrote last? Very little. Ray and Freda came over from Reading and took me out for lunch at the Anchor in Lower Froyle. That was a nice day. They are going to fetch my little sister from Minehead and deliver her into my care for Easter. Now that is very, very kind of them.

I had another publisher's rejection. Again the same old cry. They enjoyed reading it but the financial climate is still below freezing. Strange really, because the Chancellor assures me that we are fast on the road to recovery. I am fast reaching the conclusion that our Government does not know what to do next. They are on a par with Graham Gooch's boys.

What else? Oh yes! My cooker went on the blink and is

partially kaput. So I have had to buy a new one. It is being delivered next Wednesday. Cookers have gone up in price 300% since I bought the last one. A mere twenty years ago! But there, I must not complain. Man cannot live by bread alone. I must have something on which to cook my porridge.

I have one visitor next week; Cynthia is coming on Monday the eighth and returning to Nottingham on the ninth. As I have had no news of the rest of the family since January it will be a change to hear news from at least one branch of the Squire tribe.

At this stage I was interrupted.

0313 080393.

If you study these figures you will see that I could not sleep, and decided to get out of bed and continue this nonsense.

How is it that people always know when I am either upstairs on the loo or making the bed? I am sure that they stand on my doorstep and wait. Then they somehow know.

'Ah! He has gone upstairs. I'll wait a few moments and then ring the bell.'

Or is everyone psychic?

'Let's give old James a ring. Just wait till he's on the loo then dial 0420 23585.'

Everyone is trying to make me invest in one of those portable phones. I refuse. Running up and down stairs keeps me fit. I could of course have a heart attack or break a blood vessel, but then it wouldn't matter anyway, would it?

The lady-Farrier that comes to see to my feet (I can't spell 'Chiropodist') complained that she tried to ring me five times but my phone never answers. She struck lucky in the end and is coming next Thursday at 0845 hours. I hope that I shall be awake.

Can anyone tell me why people wear sunglasses in mid-winter and indoors at that? I think that it's because they have funny eyes that they wish to hide. Crossed or bloodshot! Why too, do women wear them on the top of their heads and not over their eyes? Crazy.

Another thing that puzzles me, is why no one ever lowers the lavatory seat after using the toilet. I'm sure that the seat was not designed to just be a back rest.

Have you noticed the increasingly large number of women who are appearing on our television screens? Newscasters, weather women, comediennes, sports commentators, chat show hostesses, just to name a small section. The BBC and ITV certainly have no sex-discrimination. At the current rate of female employees they will soon be accused of male discrimination.

I warned you all some letters back that the girls were taking over. I suppose I could tolerate a lady vicar more than I could a gay one.

I was recently presented with a small badge to pin on to my lapel. It had a caption printed in bold white letters on a red background:

I AM PAST IT

Wearing it I hopefully toured the village seeking some kind lady to prove it wrong.

I failed dismally. I am now resigned to the sad fact that I must be 'past it'.

Mind you, in my pure innocence I really have no idea what the 'it' can possibly refer to.

I really must stop this rambling. Perhaps I shall find some inspiration in the coming weeks.

Spring is about to be sprung. So, with a Hey! Nonny No! I must leave you.

Again,

Your 'past it' Old P.O.G.

* * *

22 March 1993

Dear All,

Spring is here. Mum's Day yesterday, and sister Hilda's eighty-seventh birthday. The sun shone.

Today it is raining. Hence this letter. However, the garden certainly needs a drink. I knew that it would rain because I cleaned the car. It is to go in for a medical check-up tomorrow so I am keeping my fingers crossed, praying that it will pass another MOT. I clean it each MOT time.

I do not find it easy to use this Amstrad PCW 8256 with my fingers crossed.

Now, what has happened since my last letter? Not a great deal to improve matters. The Chancellor presented his Budget on the sixteenth *Et tu Norman*. He stabbed me in the back again. Car tax up £15. I get caught each time. It's blackmail. He knows that people cannot exist without their wheels. Petrol up too. That means everything else will hit the roof. Cigarettes I agree with, but that is all. Beer will soon be £20 a gallon. As for the threat of VAT on household heating, well I could *****!!!!***** spit.

I shall certainly vote for Lord Sutch at the next election.

I did have a lovely day on Wednesday with Pauline and Chloe. We started at the Country Market, looked at all the bedding plants and then went on to Forest Lodge to compare prices. Coffee and doughnuts before negotiating the hazards of Laurel Grove, and a pleasant sit in the Smith Garden in the sun. Pauline gave me lunch before returning me to Bentley where I showed her the magnificent yew trees in the churchyard, and Theresa Mona's resting place in a forest of daffodils and hyacinths. We remembered to give Mrs Hollingdale her weekly peardrops to suck as she cleaned and polished the pews in the church itself. They had to leave then to go and collect Holly from school while I wended my way to the mobile library. Chloe had informed me that Sam's water bowl was dirty so I naturally had to rectify the fault. I get told off by two-year-old women now!

Thursday started on a pleasant note with a £50 from Ernie. One day he will go mad and send me the big one.

Friday was refuse day. Betty will not forget it.

She was savagely attacked by the Wheelybin as she started to propel it to the roadside ready for Biffo! It knocked her to the ground and badly sprained her hand. She was lucky not to break her wrist. If it attacks her again we shall be forced to have it put down.

Now I must wait for the medical report on the car. I can write no more with my fingers crossed. I will complete this when the result is known.

0916 240393

Susan has returned the car after its medical check-up. An expensive operation will enable it to survive for another year. It will go back into the garage next Monday. I shall recross my fingers again then.

My bedside clock with its silent alarm gave up the ghost on Sunday last. A visit to the Jeweller's in Alton was essential. I told the Saleslady that I needed an alarm. The loudest that they could produce. I removed my hearing aids, sat down and closed my eyes simulating sleep, so that they might demonstrate its clarion sound. Nothing! I am more deaf than I imagined. The sales staff were convulsed with laughter and found it difficult to believe. However, I bought it and tested it out that night. Blissfully I slept on. I rang the Saleslady after breakfast and told her that it had failed its test and that as it was under guarantee, what were they going to do? They were not helpful but at least I provided them all with a great deal of amusement. There is only one answer; I either stay asleep or hire a trumpeter to sound the reveille beside my bed each morning. One other piece of advice that I received was that I should install a flashing light by my bed but I fail to understand how I could possibly see that if I'm asleep. I like the idea of a trumpeter best.

The subject of sleep also came to my notice when I read an article in the *Radio Times* extolling the efficiency of Slumberland beds. Have you ever heard of the sleep hormone, serotonin? Neither had I until then.

A study in America (it could only happen in America) using volunteers, proved that the foods that made them drowsiest at bedtime were English muffins and bananas!

Can you picture me going to bed with a plate full of muffins and bananas? You could? You surprise me. I don't think I'm quite that mad.

There, I've waffled on again. I do trust that you will receive some benefit from all these literary gems of knowledge and advice. Now I had better do something useful.

The sun is shining now and everything in the garden is lovely and I am told that the birds are singing!

As ever,

Your deaf old P.O.G.

* * *

20 April 1993

Dear All,

April has taken its toll. I am a shadow of my former self. Albeit a somewhat corpulent shadow. Nephew Keith, when he collected his mother from my care last Sunday, pointed a camcorder at me and then showed me the result on my television screen. I had no idea that I looked so repulsively old. In future, what little of it is left, cameras, camcorders and any other recording device are strictly taboo.

The month started as usual on the first; Sam's birthday and April Fool's Day. Sam did not mind and was delighted with a present of minced lamb. He is now four years old.

It also rained. Pauline invited me to the Spring Service of Rowledge Church of England School and drove over to transport me to St James' Church. In spite of the heavy rain the Service was a great success. Poems performed by children in their first year followed by hymns and music by all the children. It really was a delightful experience and of course Holly's debut.

The rest of the week I spent preparing for the visit of Hilda Margaret who was to be delivered into my care on Tuesday the sixth. I decorated the front door with red, white and blue balloons and did hope to borrow some children from the school to wave Union Jacks but the school had broken up for Easter so I had to just have Betty to cheer. The balloons were miscontrued by some of my neighbours who thought I was celebrating my birthday and some, who imagined that I had produced triplets.

The welcome however, was a success and the subsequent lunch a hilarious feast. I excelled myself with a menu of pea and ham soup (Sainsbury's), prawn salad (Sainsbury's), a bottle of Hock (Sainsbury's), and bread and butter puddings (James special).

My guests were very flattering.

And so began the holiday of my elderly sister. Hilda began talking the moment she arrived, and only during the brief moments when she dropped off to sleep after lunch while I was washing up, did she stop. Fortunately everyone rallied round and descended to help me out.

Pauline invited us to lunch on the Wednesday, and her mother-in-law, together with assistance from Holly and Chloe, kept Hilda Margaret well and truly entertained.

Fortunately my wheels were returned having successfully passed their MOT, so I was able to chauffeur my guest around the countryside. We visited the Country Market, Forest Lodge, Farnham, Alton and on Easter Sunday, after Morning Service, I drove her over to Sunningdale for lunch at the Dairy House. The Church Service was somewhat disappointing. The church was packed but neither of us could follow or hear what was going on. However, Richard and Nicola did make the day. Hilda even received an Easter egg. So did I. Mine was engraved with the word 'GRANDAD' in white icing.

I seemed to spend many hours in the kitchen hovering over a hot stove from early morning tea in the bedroom until bedtime snacks. Hilda's appetite has not diminished with age. She tells me that she has only half a stomach! Betty as usual turned up trumps and took her out to tea with Mrs Jamieson and Kay Mason so that I might have a few moments to catch my breath. My autobiography was also brought into play and I managed to snatch a few quiet moments while Hilda was engrossed in eighty years of James. She thought it was very exciting and a much better read than Jeffrey Archer.

I bravely drove her to Guildford so that she might visit an old school-friend. A masterly bit of map reading and a dig into my recollections of the town enabled me to find No. 15 Parkhurst Road, the home of Mrs Lottie Pollard. Her first remark when she saw me was, 'Isn't he like his father?' She also added that the last time that she saw me I had an armful of books and was wearing a Grammar School cap. Now that goes back a few years. Hilda and Lottie certainly found a lot to talk about. I believe that they even made plans for a reunion in Minehead later in the year.

And so the days swiftly passed. I think Hilda enjoyed her holiday and so for that matter did I enjoy having her. I did feel somewhat limp after Keith and Janet had taken her away on the Sunday. I am getting old. No! I am old. The garden is ablaze with tulips and looks very gay.

Today Betty and I went to the Country Market and bought bedding plants, geraniums and Busy Lizzies, to replace the tulips and daffodils when they are over.

And so life goes on in dear old Bentley. New neighbours have moved in next door although I have yet to meet them.

Now I must get back into a steady routine and find out what has been going on around me.

What little I have heard from the BBC News reflects little change from the usual worldly mayhem. Worse if anything.

So once more I love you and leave you,

Your un-photogenic, worn out P.O.G.

* * *

7 May 1993

Dear All,

Here I am again and the first week of May already gone. I shouted MAYDAY! MAYDAY! MAYDAY! without success. No one came to my rescue. Of course it isn't May Day anymore. It is merely a Bank Holiday. No children dancing round Maypoles. No May Queen with her crown of flowers. All our English traditions seem to have disappeared. St George's Day, the twenty-third of April, passed without even a mention. I believe the flag of St George was flown from the church tower but that was all. It should have been flown at half mast. England is dead.

The Welsh celebrate St David's Day with daffodils, leeks and male voice choirs. The Irish proudly wear their shamrocks in honour of St Patrick. The Scots sport thistles and toast St Andrew in malt whisky but poor old St George is forgotten. The Labour Party have usurped the red rose and no one seems to care. I expect if I could do a little research I would unearth a few places in the depths of the country where a few Morris dancers still perform in his honour.

The ethnic population have an orgy of patriotism with their Notting Hill Carnival but no one, well perhaps a few lonely souls, ever thinks of England and St George.

Poor old England. Let's go to Macdonalds and have a quarter pounder washed down with a Coca-Cola or a Pepsi. Then we could go to Alton Towers or Disney Land. We might even watch *Hawaii Five-O* or *L.A. Law*. There might even be a repeat of *Dallas.* Again, we could perhaps watch *Neighbours* from Down-Under or *Home and Away*. Australians don't give a XXXX for anything else.

I suppose once we are all Europeople we might even celebrate Bastille Day, and pop over for a few bottles of French vino.

Down with the English! Enough said P.O.G. Get with it. Stop moaning. Right, I will.

A letter addressed to Maudie arrived a few days ago. I returned it inscribed 'Address Unknown'. I didn't open it in case it might have been a bill.

The only visitor I have had this month so far was the Rector. He at least found a few moments to come and cheer me up. Very busy he has been too. Inundated with funerals and sick visiting. Strangely enough I had written to him that day to wish him well with his religious conference on Saturday the eighth. He is hoping for an upsurge of fervour for the Church among backsliders in the village. I rather feel he is fighting a losing battle. My dogmatic views with a little more fire and brimstone in place of all this 'Love they Neighbour' approach might achieve something, and yet again it might not. It would probably turn away the loyal few.

One omen did occur during his visit. Sam. He came in, walked slowly to the Rector's feet, looked up and then gently jumped on to his lap and curled up. There must be something exuding from men of the cloth because he behaved exactly the same when the Bishop came to tea. Mind you I told him after the Rector had left, that sucking up to the Clergy would get him nowhere.

Now I am in the throes of preparing myself for the last, I repeat, the last Regimental Reunion of the 16th/5th The Queen's Royal Lancers Old Comrades Association on Saturday and the Cavalry Memorial Parade on Sunday. I even decided that I ought to buy a new bowler hat for the occasion. It was an unwise decision. Had I known that a new bowler would cost £96 sterling, I would have thought twice before committing myself. I hardly thought it necessary to ask for an estimate for a bowler. One lives and learns.

Today I had one pleasant surprise. A letter from my late neighbours, Peter and Linda, together with a video of their last evening in Bentley when we had a farewell dinner and Peter camcorded the event. I must have had a lot of wine to allow him to point the thing at me. I know now how repulsively old I look. He even recorded me singing (if one could term it singing) *Buttercup Joe*. No doubt it will give my immediate family a giggle. Betty of course shines, and Linda, who is the double of Mrs Amadeus Mozart in the film *Amadeus*, looks quite beautiful. But P.O.G? No! Never will I appear on film or television again. I shall start wearing dark glasses and be incognito.

Now I must stop this twaddle. I will write again when I return from London. After I have recovered of course.

Be good and pray for your decrepit old
P.O.G.

* * *

17 May 1993

Dear Children and Friends,

For the past week, ever since I returned from London after the Cavalry Memorial Parade, I have been assailed by a fit of depression. Whether it was just London, or the fact that I was closing the book on yet another page of my life, I don't know. Even visits by Angela and Pauline did little to dispel it, although I must admit that for those two days I became almost human.

Yet the weekend was a great success. John drove me up to the Royal Garden Hotel with his usual expertise. How he navigates through all that chaotic traffic if beyond me. He drove straight to the hotel as if he did it daily. Once there life was easy for me, although John I believe, had to descend miles into the earth below the hotel to park the car. He said he thought he would never stop going down. Liveried men in top hats almost carried me to the reception desk where a beautiful Japanese girl put me through all the formalities of form filling and in no time at all, I was waiting for John to return from the nether regions of the carpark. My room was on the ninth floor. I just followed John and did as I was told.

One does not have a door key now, just a card that slots in rather like a cheque card. The view from the room was fantastic; acres of park surrounding Kensington Palace. The view alone was worth the money.

We changed and dressed for the evening before wending our way down to the bar and the gathering of old comrades, and with pints of beer we were soon in a bewildering host of greetings from friends that I had not seen for years. My electric ears were so battered that I just grinned and nodded my head in a pretence that I understood what everyone was saying. I probably gave a very good picture of a senile old man but it seemed that they all politely forgave me. The dinner was really splendid with a superb menu and music from the Regimental Band while we ate and talked. And then it was all over. The last time. The last dinner of the Old Comrades Association and John was steering me upwards to the ninth floor and bed. He left me and went to catch a taxi to Fulham where he was spending the night at his daughter Rachel's flat. He was going to join me for breakfast at 8.30 a.m. I slept.

The management slipped up and I did not get my early morning tea, but I did manage to find the breakfast room by 8.30 a.m. For some strange reason, it could not possibly have been caused by the revelry of the previous evening, but I had little interest in eggs and bacon and found solace in a few cups of black coffee. John made it just after 9 a.m. He looked like a film star and was immediately surrounded by a bevy of waitresses all seeking to serve him. Unlike his father he ate everything they put before him.

I thought what a handsome efficient son I had.

He took over the reins once more and guided me through all the ritual of booking out and settling the account. He recovered the car from the bowels below and somehow found a parking space within reasonable walking distance of the Cavalry Memorial in Hyde Park. My son is a very clever chap. He was patient with me too as I puffed and staggered my way across the park to join the throng of bowler-hatted old soldiers wending their way to the parade ground. The security arrangements were amazing. I had to empty my pockets, hand over my umbrella and allow a policewoman to run a metal detector over me. My metal hips momentarily made her think that she had found a terrorist.

Then, for a space of time we stood amongst a throng of old and serving officers from every cavalry regiment with their wives, families and girlfriends chatting and waiting until the trumpeter sounded 'Fall In' and somehow we seemed to be organised into a shambled order for the march past the memorial. So I marched, no, staggered, behind the Regimental Band playing *Soldier On You Silly Bxxxxd, Soldier On!* past the Princess Royal who was taking the salute. As I removed my bowler and obeyed the 'Eyes right' command she gave me a little wave and I thought she said, 'There's old Jim,' but I couldn't be sure.

The service that followed, conducted by the Chaplain General the Reverend J Harkness CB OBE QHC MA was in truly military tradition. It was also the last that will be attended by the Regiments before amalgamation takes its toll. The rain held off until the end and the order 'Dismiss'.

And John again drove me back home. I could not have gone without him. Thanks, John.

The fact that it was the last time only really sank in after John had left me to return to Wilton.

I expect that caused my sadness.

1016 200593

You will notice that some days have elapsed since I switched off.
I have been endeavouring to shake off this fit of gloom that has
descended on me. Today it is raining so I had better put the
finishing touches to this saga of despondency. A letter today
tells me that even the Regimental Band is being dis-banded. I
hate all politicians.

Even the garden refuses to germinate any real enthusiasm
although I force myself to refurbish it after the spring flowers
have died. Maudie will only arrive to stick pins in me if I lapse.
Betty made me go up to St Mary's Church and tidy up. We
removed the dead bulbs and replanted with geraniums. At least
Betty did. I stood by and puffed.

I think perhaps that the two days when Angela and Pauline
came cheered me up, but a few moments watching the BBC
News soon dispelled any feeling of *joie de vivre*. If they go on like
this I shall become the 'Complete Pessimist'. Poor old England.
We really are going through a bad patch.

I am going to cease this diatribe and have a chat to Sam. He
does not worry about anything.

Perhaps June will see a resurge in my spirits.

A rum and dry ginger will no doubt help.

So until then just give the odd thought to
                    Your grumpy old P.O.G.

                    * * *

                                                    1 June 1993

Dear All,

May is out. You can cast as many clouts as you wish. I am glad
May is out. It was not my best month. At least not until the last
two or three days.

I sat on my glasses. My driving glasses. I had to dash down to

90

the opticians. I paid heavily for my stupid carelessness. And my house-martins have not returned this summer. They were due on the twenty-first of May. Last year we must have had half a dozen or more pairs nesting but this year only about three pairs have made it back. My nests under the eaves have been let to a family of belligerent sparrows. I suppose the poor house-martins ran into trouble somewhere on their return journey from Africa, or wherever they spent the winter.

Anyway June is now here. At least this first day has been up to standard. I even did some tidying up in the garden. The Spring Bank Holiday was enlivened by visits from my old neighbours Peter and Linda, together with their charming children Megan and Jeffrey. It is wonderful to be visited by someone so full of vitality and gaiety. They have the ability to make life seem fun. A very rare achievement in these troublesome times. Peter was collecting his bicycle and we saw him off on his ride to Grantham. I am waiting now to know how he got on. I did offer him a bottle of Elliman's Horse Liniment, which I am sure he must have needed after the first seventy miles. He turned my offer down!

The neighbour who moved in after them has decided that living in the green and pleasant land is too difficult and has upsticked and returned to Ireland. So again I am neighbour-less.

Postcard time is here again. One from Scotland depicting the usual River Dee tells me that John has caught an eight and a half pound salmon. Richard and Nicola are sampling Guinness somewhere in Southern Ireland. Richard says, I quote: 'Natives say we may have a long wait for the rain to clear! Spectacular scenery (we're told) but visibility rarely over forty yards!'

I can't understand why they don't spend their short breaks in sunny old Bentley. Who on earth wants bogs, bagpipes, leprechauns, four-leaf-clovers and blarney stones? Richard and Nicola of course!

Now June. Derby Day and the start of the First Test Match. It is raining at Old Trafford and England will avoid defeat. It will no doubt give me a topic for discussion. Actually I am giving thought to an article in the *Radio Times* on faith by Polly Toynbee.

She says that she is an 'unbeliever'. By that I take it that she did once believe but has since become unned. Otherwise I feel she would have said that the was a non-believer. She also states that only a few children know the essential Bible stories. I wonder what she means by the essential Bible stories? It's an idea. I might pick some of the best out for her.

Let's start at the beginning: Genesis.

'In the beginning God created the heaven and the earth.' He must have worn his fingers to the bone. He did it in six days and then sat back to rest on the seventh. He made Adam in his own image and planted him in the garden of Eden and then made his first mistake. He took one of Adam's ribs and made a woman. He also warned him not to eat the fruit of the tree of life that was growing in the centre of the garden. And Adam called the woman Eve. There was also in the garden a wicked reptile who used his wiles on Eve and persuaded her to pick the fruit of the forbidden tree and offer it to Adam. It was probably a Cox's Orange. Anyway, Adam took a bite and immediately saw that he was naked and taking a decco at Eve saw that she was naked as well. They both became embarrassed and went dashing off looking for something to cover their whatsits. Only fig leaves were big enough.

And God was angry with them. He was angry with the serpent too, and put a curse on it to make it slither on its belly from that day on. That's where the phrase snake in the grass comes from. Eve was too busy sewing fig leaves together to be worried. The first fashion show was held in the Garden of Eden. And God was really very, very cross and turned them out of the Garden of Eden and put a lot of unpleasant curses on them because they had started knowing good and evil. And they had the choice. So if Eve hadn't scrumped that Cox's apple the world might have been a better place. Anyway it didn't stop there. Adam and Eve had two sons, Cain and Abel. Abel was the keeper of the sheep and Cain was the tiller of the ground. It was Cain who blotted his copy book. He knocked his brother off and God was not at all pleased.

He banished Cain to the land of Nod which was east of Eden and Cain was terrified that everyone would try to take revenge on him and kill him. But God did not want him killed, and put a mark on him and said that anyone killing him would be cursed sevenfold. It became known as the Mark of Cain. Anyway, Cain survived and had a son called Enoch and he built a city and named it after his son. And that's where it all started, and Enoch begat Irad, and Irad begat Mehujael, and the begatting really started. One after the other. Methuselah lived 187 years and begat Lamech, and then after that lived 782 years and begat sons and daughters. And all the days of Methuselah were 969 years. And he died. Then you can keep on and even up to Noah. They all lived for hundreds of years in those days.

It is all very complicated and they didn't have computers then so all that was handed down from word of mouth and probably got a bit mixed up in the telling.

Anyway, it was that lot that started all the wickedness in the world and God began to have second thoughts about what He had started and it grieved Him to see all that evil and He decided to rub it out and start again.

I shall have to tell you about that later.

I expect you will find my theology a little difficult to understand but if you read the Book of Genesis I doubt that you will find it any easier.

I'd better stop. To think that it was Polly Toynbee who started this train of thought. Women again.

Farewell for now,

Your idiotic P.O.G.

* * *

27 June 1993

Dear All,

It is all over. It is the end. On Friday the twenty-fifth of June the history book was closed on the 16th/5th The Queen's Royal Lancers and the 17th/21st Lancers.

Although it was a memorable day that none of those present will ever forget, it was one of mixed emotions; the pleasure of meeting so many old friends, some that I had not seen for forty years, and the overwhelming sadness that it would never happen again.

The day started with Angela driving me over to Wilton where we were to transfer to John's car for the journey to Bulford Camp for the parade. Angela, Taffy, Emma and Rachel all looked absolutely beautiful in their Ascot style outfits. Without a doubt, John and I accompanied the four most elegant ladies of the day. It was a gorgeous day. Glorious June with Heaven-sent breeze. We found our seats in the stands surrounding the parade ground. Angela and I had to sit with all the ancients, while John and his family sat in a stand with serving officers. We were early and had the opportunity to meet and chat with so many old friends before the arrival of Her Majesty. Then the Amalgamation Parade began. I shall not describe the parade itself although it was a fautless demonstration of drill. I hope that I shall be able to get a copy of the film at a later date. The Queen as usual looked absolutely wonderful.

The old colours were marched from the parade. The new colours after a Service of Consecration were presented by Her Majesty and trooped by the new Regiment, The Queen's Royal Lancers.

The only 'hiccup' in the whole day, at least as far as I was concerned, was during a drive past of historic vehicles. This was led by two Lancers, one 16th and one 17th, mounted on horses which I am sorry to say bore no resemblance to any cavalry horses of my experience. They were awful. The accoutrements were appalling. Scruffy civilian saddles and bridles quite out of place with Lancers in dress uniforms.

I was reminded of a sketch I saw once of Don Quixote and his man Pancho. I visualised a great turning of old cavalrymen in their graves. What Her Majesty thought I dread to think. They could have so easily borrowed properly-dressed horses from the Military Police. But perhaps no one else noticed it. Maybe I was the only man there to have known a mounted regiment. It was my only criticism of the whole day.

The parade over, we made our way to the royal lunch marquee while the Queen was joining her new regiment for photographs. This was a period before the lunch when we met old friends and comrades. The difficulty was placing names to faces from the past.

The lunch itself was splendid and over only too soon with royal toasts and a brief speech by the Colonel-in-Chief.

And then we were wending our way back to the cars and a brief stay with John and Taffy before the short journey back to Tollard Royal.

John, like myself, was conscious of a feeling of great sadness. John probably more than me. He was taking his uniform off for the last time. He even wore my hat on the parade. He will soon be leaving Her Majesty's Service and entering this civilian rat-race and I know only too well how difficult the transition can be. Both he and Taffy will miss the *esprit de corps* found only in a regiment like ours.

Now I am back in dear old Bentley thinking about another birthday. I wonder how many more.

I have new neighbours. Strange ones. Asians whom I have yet to see. They live enclosed, with windows tight shut and curtains drawn. They have a baby because I glimpsed it and have heard its cries. They put washing out on the line but I never see them. Perhaps they are invisible. I think they are connected to the Army and that the house has been taken over by the Military. But I don't really know. I shall have to leave it to my more inquisitive friends to find out.

Now I must stop. I said that I would continue with my theological stories and I am due to embark on the generations of Noah but I really have to be in the right frame of mind for such an undertaking. Perhaps I'll add a P.S. when I have the urge.

Be good,

As ever,

P.O.G.

P.S.

I have just seen the lady next door. She is a dusky maiden dressed in a sari and very pretty. I need not now be worried about the baby because I'm sure she cares for it properly. I wonder if I shall ever know her name?

7 July 1993

Dear Children and Friends,

Flaming June has gone. Ascot, and a bevy of ladies in ridiculous hats, short skirts and bony knees paraded their charms for an equally ridiculous lady 'fashion' commentator to enthuse over. The weather was kind only for the first two days. The Queen looked lovely and the horses and jockeys made the days exciting. I picked out a loser in each race that I watched.

Wimbledon will be remembered as the year without rain. Glorious sunshine for the whole fortnight and the BBC was tennis-tennis-tennis for eight hours non-stop each day with highlights of the day's play for a bonus later in the evening. I watched the odd game just to keep in touch and see who was winning. I must ring my sister and find out who did.

The Third Test Match started at Trent Bridge and Captain Gooch and his boys fought their way to a draw. In fact they nearly won. The 'Down-Unders' put on their face paint, combed their bewhiskered faces and put on a determined attack. Why do I find them so revolting? Especially the fast bowler Merv Hughes? But then I am rather anti 'Down-Unders', tired of *Home and Away*, *Neighbours*, and pictures of a 'Holiday of a Lifetime' in the countless quiz shows that monopolise the box.

The Opera House and Sydney Bridge seem to permanently invade the screen.

'The Lions' have at least kept the Union Jack flying in the world of rugby.

Perhaps the tragic death of my regiment in that last week made me over critical of the other June events.

And now it is July. The month of Leo.

The word 'holiday' is on every tongue. Parents can't wait for the kids to finish school.

Conversations are all the same:

'Where are you going this year?'

'Oh! We're going to the Greek Islands. Where are you off to?'

96

'We've got a 'time-share' in the South of France. We went to Tunisia last year but the heat was appalling and nothing but sand and flies. Dreadful!'

And so on and so on. Everywhere in the world except dear old England. No sun. Only rain. No topless bathing. Boring.

Not quite true because I saw a picture of topless belles in Bournemouth of all places.

Anyway what's wrong with rain? There's nothing more pleasant than to feel rain gently beating into one's face. I remember once, out walking with a beautiful girl. It was along the Pilgrim's Way and we got caught in a heavy shower. We sheltered under a great oak and she suddenly looked up at me and said, 'You know you look quite handsome with rain on your face.'

It just goes to prove that rain can even mesmerise beautiful girls. I nearly, but not quite, proposed to her.

I remember too, reading somewhere at the beginning of a novel:

'It's the hard grey weather that breeds hard Englishmen.'

Now they all go to the Bahamas and all points north, south, east and west so we finish up with a load of softees.

Anyway there will soon be no Englishmen. The word itself is almost extinct.

'Brits' is the term now. I find it quite insulting. I do not want to be a Brit. I just want to stay English.

I wonder if any of you remember the play that we saw on Susan's twenty-first birthday?

Dear Octopus by Dodie Smith. I think he was the author. Drury Lane Theatre with Jack Hulbert and Cicely Courtenage as the mum and dad with everyone turning up for an anniversary.

He might have been writing about our family, and I for one shall be thinking of it on the twenty-sixth day of the month when you all join me for a party. I only wish Maud could have been with us.

My invitation did cause a little trouble with one prospective guest. I signed it 'James Squire P.O.G.'

They spent the whole evening searching the dictionaries to find out what honour or decoration the letters P.O.G. stood for.

97

They thought it was some obscure military medal.

'Professor of Gunnery'?

They nearly exploded when I told them it was 'Poor Old Grandad'.

So with that I shall leave you and trust that you have all got your passages booked for Disney Land.

As ever,

Your anglophile P.O.G.

* * *

13 July 1993

Dear Children and Friends,

This is not a letter. Well, not a letter for distribution, except to those who ask for it.

My sister, Hilda Margaret, and I are the only people that I know who write letters. The one I received from her this morning was even written at the expense of a saucepan and an egg. She left it on the stove with heat on full, heard a large explosion and found a ruined saucepan and no egg. However I do not think that this could be the reason why so few of my family have time to write letters.

Why does no one write letters? Is it because they are not taught during their educational years?

Are they not taught to spell? Is syntax a forgotten subject? It can't be because they have not the time. They have washing machines, refrigerators, washing-up machines, microwave ovens, fast food, telelphones, answerphones, fax machines; in fact every time-saving device that man can conjure up. Out of 168 hours in each week they only work forty hours. What do they do with the other 126 hours? They each have a motor car to save them wasting time walking. Anyway, whatever the reason the Postman has little to do except put junk mail through my letter box.

Hurrah for sister Hilda Margaret!

She even wishes me to continue with my theology and tell her about Noah. A difficult task but for her I will try.

Turn to Genesis 6 v.5

'And God saw that the wickedness of man was great
in the Earth'.

To put it in simple English he was cheesed-off with the
debauchery and goings on of the generations of Adam. In fact
he was so cheesed-off that he decided to knock them all off and
start again. (See v.7)

But Noah found grace in the eyes of the Lord who decided to
put Noah in charge. He instructed him to build an ark and told
him how to do it. He was to use gopher wood and make it three
hundred cubits long, fifty cubits wide and thirty cubits high. He
even told him where to put the windows and doors.

Then He made Noah the first conservationist and told him to
collect up a male and female of all the animals and birds that he
could find. And all the creepy crawlies. So Noah and his sons,
Shem, Ham and Japheth got cracking. You will find a good
description of that in Genesis 7 vs. 1 & 2.

Noah was 600 years old at this time. God then told him to get
aboard with all his goods and chattels and it started to rain.
Believe me it really did rain. It drowned every living thing that
was on the earth except Noah and his lot who were now sailing
merrily along. Everything was flooded for 150 days and the
generations of Adam were destroyed. God was pretty angry
with that lot.

On the seventh of July Noah found himself stuck on the top of
Mount Ararat until the first of October, when God pulled the
plug out and let the waters subside.

Then old Noah opened the window and sent forth a raven
which went forth to and fro until the water dried up. He then let
loose a pigeon – sorry, dove, but it could not find anywhere to
roost, so it flew back and Noah waited for another week before
he sent it off again. This time it came back with an olive leaf in its
beak and Noah knew that the earth was back to normal, but it
was a long time before God told him to disembark and, 'Go forth
from the Ark, thou and thy wife and thy sons and their wives
with them.'

So Noah let all the animals loose and they went forth also

And the Lord blessed Noah and his sons and said unto them 'Be fruitful and multiply; and replenish the Earth,' and He also promised that He would not interfere with man again, but leave him to his own devices.

And so started the generations of Noah which as you will know did not do much better than the generations of Adam.

Noah himself blotted his copybook by planting a vineyard and getting sloshed with his first brew. God was not pleased. Noah was the first alcoholic, but he still lived 350 years after the flood and all the days of Noah were 950 years. And he died.

Shem and Ham and Japheth carried on and I quote, 'of them was the whole earth overspread.'

And a right mess they made of it too.

We shall study their goings-on next. (I said that this was not a letter for distribution so I shall print it only for Hilda Margaret and my file.)

Your foolishly theological P.O.G.

P.S.

If you are interested – a cubit is 18 in. to 22 in. – the length of a forearm. So the Ark must have been about 150 yds. long, 24 yds. wide and 15 yds. high. It still must have been somewhat crowded.

* * *

17 July 1993

Dear All,

It rained on St Swithin's Day and it's raining today. So I suppose I shall have to put up with it for forty days and forty nights. I've also got a stinking, chesty cold and I am fed up. I might just as well amuse myself with the further generations of Noah.

Not that I know much about what Noah himself got up to after he did his bit with the Ark. We know that he lived for a few hundred years after that. We also know that he made a long covenant with God which was full of dos and don'ts. We also know that he went into the wine business and his sons found him well and truly sloshed up, but there seems to be no more records of him doing anymore begatting after he produced Shem, Ham and Japheth. Perhaps he spent the rest of his days treading on the old grape and tasting a few new vintages.

Mind you, it would seem that his sons did their bit. They were told to get on with populating the earth so begatting must have been their main occupation.

They did however, at one stage, decide to build a tower up to Heaven which was probably their biggest mistake because God saw it and came down to see what they were up to. He found them all talking in the same language. I had better do a quote here:

> Chapter 11 V.5
> And the Lord came down to see the city and the tower which the children of men had builded.
>
> And the Lord said, behold, the people is one, and they have all one language.
>
> Go to, let us go down, and there confound their language, that they may not understand one another's speech.
>
> So the Lord scattered them abroad from thence upon the face of the earth . . . .

And the place became known as the 'Tower of Babel'.

I don't know why God objected to them using the same language but he certainly put the cat among the pigeons.

You will find a prime example of Babel in the Brussels European Parliament. No one there knows what the chap next door is saying. They all shake hands and grin and look frightfully knowledgeable. It is not easy to converse using an interpreter.

I remember teaching a class of Polish officers. I asked a question which the interpreter translated into Polish. I indicated the officer who was to answer. He grinned and answered in fluent Polish. He went on and on until I said stop.

'What does he say?' I asked.

'He says that he doesn't know.'

And I expect that is what goes on in Brussels.

But I am getting away from Shem, Ham and Japheth.

It was then that the begatting really began. I can't write it all down but it went on for generations.

Example:

> V.11 And Shem lived after he begat Arphaxad five hundred years, and begat sons and daughters.

Mind you there was a lot of earth to be populated and they certainly started a lot of new tribes.

I shall concentrate on just a few of the more important characters like Abraham and Lot who were the offsprings of Terah. It was Terah who took them into the land of Canaan where they lived until he died when he was a mere 205.

It was at this stage that God blessed Abraham and promised to make him a great nation. There was a lot of mucking about then and because there was a famine in the land, Abraham decided to take a short break in Egypt. Now Sarai, Abraham's wife, although she was barren, was very beautiful and Abraham got worried that if the Egyptians knew that she was his wife they would knock him off and take her for themselves so he pretended that she was his sister.

The Egyptians went all gaga over Sarai and she was taken into Pharaoh's house and they entreated Abraham well for her sake, and he had sheep and oxen, and he-asses and men-servants, and she-asses and maid-servants and camels. And altogether he was on to a good thing.

But God was not having it. He plagued Pharaoh with great plagues because of Sarai, and poor old Pharaoh got quite niggled. He tore Abraham off a right strip for deceiving him and told him to shove off back to where he came from. Abraham was over the moon because by now he was very rich in cattle, in silver and gold and wasted no time in heading north. He took

Sarai and Lot, who by this time were also loaded down with flocks and herds, and he pitched his tents in a place called Bethel.

He still had his troubles though. His men fell out with Lot's men and they were heading for a right old bust-up. Abraham did not want strife between him and Lot so they agreed to split up with Lot, choosing to move to the fertile plain of Jordan while Abraham stayed in Canaan.

And Lot pitched his tents toward Sodom.

Now comes the crunch:

Chapter 13 v.13.

> But the men of Sodom were wicked and sinners before the Lord exceedingly.

If you want to know that happened next wait until the next instalment. I'm exhausted.

It has also stopped raining.

As ever,

Your P.O.G.

* * *

23 July 1993

Dear All,

I still have not shaken off this filthy cold. I only wish that I knew who deposited the germ and then I would be able to invoke a horrible punishment on the culprit. I'm sure it's all this kissing lark. Women dashing up to plant their germ ridden lips on my innocent face.

I only hope that I have got rid of it before my birthday next Monday or you will all be celebrating without me.

I would also like to know why I have got involved in biblical research. It was that stupid Polly Toynbee in the *Radio Times* and her unbelieving attitude. Now I am hooked. I did not realise how little I knew. The Bible ain't the easiest book to read. I think the main difficulty is trying to visualise the map of the earth as it was then. My geography was based on all the red bits on the map before we gave the Empire away and now that they all have independence they have changed all the names so that I don't know where any of my old red bits have got to. It's all very confusing.

I suppose that if I were to do a little more research I am sure that the archaeologists have sorted it all out and I see that one can even take a holiday through biblical Jordan. I did once visit the Hanging Gardens Of Babylon but I was not impressed. I was escorted by a very knowledgeable priest who even pointed out Nebuchadnezzar's Banquet Hall. It just looked like a heap of sand to me and there was certainly nothing growing or hanging in the garden.

Perhaps religion, like politics, is best left alone.

And where did I leave poor old Lot? I remember. He has pitched his tents at Sodom. It was not a wise move. He got mixed up in a war. Four neighbouring kings decided to make war against the King of Sodom and the King of Gomorah and poor old Lot was on the losing side. I pictured it something like the nonsense going on in Yugoslavia at the moment between the Serbs, Croats and Bosnians. The causes were probably much the same. The only difference being the fact in those days they fought with charriots, bows and arrows, and spears, while modern conflicts use tanks, helicopter gunships and Kalishnikov rifles. Anyway, read . . . Chapter 14 v.11

> And they took all the goods of Sodom and Gomorah, and all their victuals, and went their way.
>
> And they took Lot, Abram's brother's son, and his goods, and departed.
>
> And there came one that escaped, and told Abram the Hebrew.

Abram wasn't having that. He mobilised his servants and went off to the rescue. He smote the opposition and rescued Lot and his goods, and the women also, and the people. The King of Sodom was more than grateful but Abram refused any reward, 'not even from a thread even to a shoelatchet'. And Lot was back in Sodom where it all started.

Abram went back home, had a lot of visions, made another covenant with the Lord and was promised a 'numerous seed'.

This however, was a little awkward because Sarai, his wife, was barren. Sarai solved the problem. She took her maid, Hagar the Egyptian, and gave her to Abram to be his wife and to cut a long story short, Hagar produced them a son named Ishmael.

After that, the Lord promised Abram that Sarai would bear him a son but he had to change her name from Sarai to Sarah and the child was to be called Isaac. It was around this time that for some reason, which is beyond me, all male children had to be circumcised. Not only the children, Abram himself and all the men of his household.

Anyway, the Lord blessed Abram, now called Abraham, and promised that he would become a 'great and mighty nations'.

All this time Lot was still at his tents at Sodom which was not a nice place. In fact it was very wicked. The Lord did not approve and decided that they would have to be taught a lesson.

Sodom of course was where our current 'gay' fraternity got all their ideas from. They should have kept the title, 'Sodomites' not ruined a nice word like 'gay'.

Anyway Old Nick had been busy spreading vice and wickedness and the Lord decided that the Sodomites ought to be taught a lesson. Mind you, all the people living in Sodom were not wicked, some were quite righteous and Abraham pleaded with God not to include them in the punishment and did a lot of bargaining on their behalf.

It seems that two angels paid Lot a visit and a lot of arguing took place between Lot and the people, and when the morning came they told Lot to upsticks and take his wife and two daughters out of it lest they be consumed in the iniquity of the city. They also warned him not to look behind him and hightail it to the mountains which he did, just in time.

Ch. 19 v.24

The Lord rained down upon Sodom and upon
Gomorah brimstone and fire from the Lord out of
Heaven.

But Lot's wife could not resist it. She had to look back and she
was turned into a pillar of salt. I can't think or find out why it
should be salt. Anyway Lot was afraid to live in Zoar, the city
that he arrived at, and he went up into the mountains and lived
in a cave with his two daughters.

Now a bit more jiggery-pokery started.

The elder daughter said unto the younger, 'Our father
is old and he is the only man around these parts. We
will ply him with wine and we will lie with him that
we may preserve the seed of our father.'

So they get old Lot sloshed and took it in turn to get him
begatting and both the daughters of Lot were with child by their
father. The elder bore a son and called his name Moab and he
became the father of all the Moabites. The younger girl
produced Benammi who became the father of the children of
Ammon.

There. What do you make of all that? It certainly is very
difficult to work out.

I wonder if I have got it all wrong. You must read it up and
correct me if I have.

No more now. I've got to start preparing myself for this
birthday party next week.

See you all then if I can make it.

As ever,

P.O.G.

*   *   *

Dear All,

What a momentous month this July of 1993 has been and now as it draws to a close I must write and thank you all for the magnificent efforts you made to make my eightieth birthday a part of history. I could never hope to thank you all enough for the profusion of gifts and cards that you showered on me.

I am a very lucky old Grandad.

My birthday really started on the twenty-fifth with the arrival of my dear old friend Major Berty Starr and Rona. They arrived in time for a high tea with wine to take the place of the traditional beverage. Berty and I talked into the small hours reminiscing on how from 1940 onwards, we won the War and how I mechanised the Royal Tank Regiment.

On birthday morning, after a leisurely breakfast, we drove over to the Country Market, with Betty to keep Rona company. They could not resist buying trays of Busy Lizzies and a variety of other colourful plants so that the car looked like a florist's delivery van. Then we motored on to the Forest Lodge Garden Centre where we browsed, partook of a snack lunch and purchased another array of potted plants.

Arriving back at No. 17 Eggars Field I found the front doorway festooned with balloons and the words 'Congratulations' pinned above the porch. The house had been entered via the back windows and a great heap of presents deposited in the chairs. Only Nicola and Richard could have been the culprits.

Then the excitement of undoing parcels.

A CENTURY SURVIVAL KIT – KEEPS OCTO-GENARIANS GOING TO 2000 AD.
* PRACTICAL ADVICE.
* TOOLS.
* RATIONS.
* PATENT CURES FOR SUNDRY AILMENTS.
'INDISPENSABLE FOR THE OVER EIGHTIES.'

I could not attempt here to describe the contents but it will be available for inspection whenever you wish to see it.

Then in the midst of all this hilarious unpacking the doorbell heralded a visit from Pauline with my greatest fans, Holly and Chloe. How refreshing it is in this day and age to be visited by two beautiful, charming and lively young ladies together with a lovely mum. It was one of the highlights of my day.

The doorbell seemed to be constantly ringing with deliveries of gifts and good wishes.

And then before I knew it, came the time to make myself presentable and hie away to the Anchor Inn at Lower Froyle to welcome my guests to supper.

It was the start of a memorable evening. I became quite dizzy. Fortunately I was able to delegate a great deal of the welcoming on to the shoulders of Richard and John.

David and Angela, Richard and Nicola, John and Taffy, Susan and Phillip, Hermione and Roger, only Michael and Mary missing, unable to come because of Mary's illness. My favourite people all together.

The Rector, Bill Rogers and Sylvia arrived to provide me religious cover. Sister Eileen Rawlings, our district nurse was to provide medical cover, but regretfully phoned to say that she was indisposed. But I was able to rest in the knowledge that Major General David Roberts, Her Majesty's late Professor of Military Medicine, was available should I need assistance.

Military cover was provided by Colonel John Squire of The Queen's Royal Lancers with back up, should he need it, from Major Berty Starr of the Royal Tank Regiment and Major Toni Rudin in charge of the Artillery. I also understand that Wing Commander Allan Pentycross had a couple of Spitfires on standby. So I knew that all my guests were safe.

As my friends all assembled the crescendo of voices rose to, for me, an undecipherable pitch so that I became even dizzier. But it was a wonderful feeling to see all my family and friends so together in gaiety and laughter.

Dear Octopus in real life and I thought how the tentacles of Kathleen Mary and Theresa Mona were somehow still with me. How they would have loved it.

Everyone was wonderful and somehow, in a muddle, they all fitted themselves into the dining room where we stood while the Reverend Bill said Grace before we started the splendid birthday supper provided by the culinary skills of Mr and Mrs Howard and presented to us by Mrs Jenkins and her young lady. Neither Mrs Beeton nor Delia Smith could have equalled it.

My ears prevented me from hearing what everyone was saying, but from my position at the head of the table my eyes assured me that all my guests were enjoying themselves.

Then it was all over. David gave a speech, which I thought so flattering that I almost blushed, and I, in return, read out my letter of congratulations from Her Majesty.

I can't understand why they all laughed.

Altogether it was a wonderful evening and no one could have had a better eightieth birthday among so many friends and a wonderful family.

It was an example of what the 'Family' is really all about.

Then Berty was driving me back home where Richard and Nicola, John and Taffy, Susan and Phillip, Hermione and Roger, Toni and Heather, Berty and Rona, Betty and Wendy and, if I remember rightly, my godaughter Jacqueline, all continued to celebrate.

By this time I was becoming somewhat confused. I vaguely remembered surfacing on the morn of the twenty-seventh. I believe Hermione and Roger together with their John and Ann, came to say goodbye before driving off to Devon just as we were finishing breakfast.

Berty and Rona drove off after lunch in a southerly direction. I had a phone conversation with my niece Thelma, who rang from Australia, and now Sam and I are recuperating and gathering strength, with assistance from the 'Century Survival Kit', to face the rest of 1993.

Sam is delighted that it is all over and that No. 17 is back to normal. We toasted absent friends and thought of Michael and Mary who could not be with us. We pray for a return to health for Mary.

Now it just remains for me to say, 'Thank you all for a wonderful birthday.'

Your proud and humble P.O.G.

*   *   *

16 August 1993

Dear All,

After all the excitements of July, August did not start on a good note.

To begin with, I dropped one of my favourite glass jugs onto the kitchen floor where it disintegrated into a million pieces.

'It slipped out of me 'and, Sir.'

A further piece of utter carelessness happened in Farnham when I went shopping. Returning to my car after completing my purchases, I discovered that the car keys were still in the ignition and I was locked out.

Idiot! Nincompoop! I called myself a variety of uncomplimentary names. I returned to the Safeway store and located the local burglar who, with obviously practised skills and a thin piece of wire, opened the door more easily than I can do it with the proper key. I was so angry with myself that I collected Betty and took her to the Anchor Inn so that I might recover my calm with a pint or so of Hardy Country Ale.

Things always happen in threes.

For some weeks I had been thinking that I should clean the filter on the washing machine but I kept putting it off.

'I'll do it next time'! No! I'll do it now. I did. You will never guess what happened.

The moment that I released the cover, a flood of water burst forth in a great deluge all over the kitchen floor. It took me hours to mop up.

I slapped my wrist and have now resolved to be more careful in future.

And so passed the first two weeks of August. The fourteenth arrived; Wedding Day for my dear goddaughter Jacqueline. She was going to be joined in Holy Matrimony to her Marc at the quaint little church of St Andrews in the tiny village of Great Linford which has, during the past few years, been absorbed

110

into the great complex of Milton Keynes.

Richard and Nicola had kindly undertaken the task of delivering me to the church on time. It would take, so I was told, about two hours. Allowing an extra thirty minutes to be on the safe side, they collected me at 9.30 a.m. on that glorious, sunny August day.

All went according to plan until we had negotiated the M3 and the M25 and were humming up the M1. A sign appeared.

ROAD WORKS. WIDENING AND RESURFACING
BETWEEN JUNCTIONS 9 and 10.

The tailback began around Junction 7. Three lanes of cars, buses and lorries all moving in fits and starts at 3 mph. Thousands of them stretching as far as the eye could see, all crawling along under a haze of carbon monoxide fumes. My driver and navigator began to get worried. They were not going to get me to the church on time.

A hasty look at the map. Leave the M1 and move on to the A5.

'Don't worry James. We'll make it yet.'

I was lost. I had not a clue where we were. I saw a sign to Milton Keynes. At least we were heading in the right direction. Then we were not. We were obviously straying. Richard pulled into the kerbside to study the map. Nicola dismounted and sought help in a nearby shop.

We were back on the right road and the clock ticked on.

Milton Keynes seventeen miles. It was fifteen minutes to twelve.

Ah! The village of Great Linford. I see no church! We enquire from a passerby. We are there!

James dismounted. The wedding was still in progress.

I waved a hasty and rather rude thank you to R and N and staggered into the little church making a rather loud entry by falling over a chair. At least it let the congregation know that I had arrived.

Jacqueline and Marc were at the chancel steps and a priestess,

111

I assume that is the correct term, was completing her address. I had only missed the first hymn which, from the Order of Service that I collected from a table by the door, I saw had been *He who would valiant be . . .* which I thought was very appropriate.

I was able to join in *The Lord's my shepherd, I'll not want,* sung to Grimmond and I thought of Theresa Mona. Grimmond was one of her unfavourite tunes. I joined in the prayers and having by this time collected my breath was able to add my vocal talents to the singing of *Praise my soul, the King of Heaven*; again the words of which I felt were in keeping with my condition . . . 'ransomed, healed, restored, forgiven'.

The priestess intoned the Blessing and I stood and watched Jacqueline, who, I must add, looked quite ravishing in her bridal dress, and Marc as they came arm in arm down the aisle to the tune of Mendelssohn's Wedding March from *A Midsummer Night's Dream.*

The whole of the Rudin family then took me in hand.

Elizabeth and Glenn together with their Thomas who was a pageboy, Simon and his lovely wife, Toni and Heather, and Fenella who was to be my mentor and guardian. It was then photographs under the magnificent trees in the lovely surrounds of the church. I was introduced to Marc's parents whose English was fortunately much better than my French.

Fenella and Mike, her handsome boyfirend, steered me to a luxurious car and with little effort on my part I was soon sitting with Fenella beside me, in their very pleasant garden with a much needed restorative glass of wine at my lips.

Fenella saved my life. It was all laughter and gaiety. A wonderful family all together and I felt a part of it.

Before I knew it, Richard and Nicola arrived to take me back to Bentley. We watched Jacqueline and Marc drive off to start their married life together before we made our farewells. Kate, who had been collected by her parents from Northampton, navigated, and avoiding motorways soon had me back home. Richard and Nicola must have been exhausted.

I was. I slept the sleep of all sleeps.

It was the end of a memorable day.

Now next Sunday is the christening of Oliver Mark Jenner in

our own village church of St Mary's.

I will tell you of that in my next letter.

As ever,

Your P.O.G.

*   *   *

Dear All,

August is drawing to a close. The great last Bank Holiday of the year is upon us. The exodus begins today. The motorways will be chockablock. The ferries to France will be laden down to the plimsol line.

I shall be sitting quietly in my garden with a few bottles of wine and a mental picture of the M1 and all the other Ms before me. And I shall think how lucky I am.

Actually the last two weeks of the month have been quite exciting if one can forget the horrors and mayhem of Bosnia and all the other trouble spots in the world.

The last two weeks started with a strange mystery.

I was taking my daily constitutional amble round the village and was negotiating the footpath beneath the walls of Jenkyns Place when a small round white object dropped from the sky in front of me a mere inch or so from my nose. A golf ball. I picked it up and printed on it was: 'Blacknest Range'.

As the Blacknest Golf Club is some three miles distant even Nick Faldo could not have made a drive of such magnitude. Perhaps it has started raining golf balls. Perhaps a magpie had picked it up and dropped in on me. I have no idea where it came from.

Anyway, I put it away in my pocket and the back of my mind and became glued to the magnificent performances of British athletes in Stuttgart. Linford Christie's success in the one hundred metres. Colin Jackson breaking the world record in the one hundred metre hurdles. John Regis winning Silver in the two hundred metres. The young high jumper and the javelin thrower and the relay teams. And for me the thrilling four

113

hundred metre hurdles with an English girl flying home to break the world record. Sally Gunnel's incredible race was for me the greatest athletic achievement since Roger Bannister ran the first four-minute mile. What a week it was.

Then to crown it all England won the Sixth Test Match at the Oval. They kept me biting my nails until the last dying moments. Mr Merv Hughes' moustache drooped even lower and the Australian face-paint paled whiter than white.

Sunday the twenty-second marked the christening of Oliver Mark Jenner in our lovely church of St Mary's. I have never attended a christening like it.

Betty and I drove up in good time and procured seats at the back where we could be sure of viewing the font. The little church then began to fill with families and friends from far and wide. They all seemed to have children of their own who decided to turn the place into an adventure playground. I began to wonder how the rector would ever manage to perform the ceremony. I was reminded of Tom Sharpe's novel *Riotous Assembly*.

The parents lost complete control. One small young lady did her best to climb into the font itself. Another tried to climb the large candlestick and blow out the flame. I noticed another young man up in the pulpit and one father retrieving an offspring from beneath the altar. The Reverend Bill and the young Oliver Mark seemed to be the only ones in the ceremony. Oliver Mark was splendid and somehow among all the din the Reverend Bill managed to baptise him. The congregation from what I could see, were only interested in taking photographs and camcorder records.

The religious portent of it all seemed to be lost in a confusion of movement and the shrill voices of children.

Then, with the ceremony over, we all descended on No. 3 Broadlands Close where Gill and Adrian had prepared a magnificent baptismal feast. The weather was kind allowing the garden to be used to the full.

My deaf ears were again assailed by a crescendo of voices. I really am not built for parties.

To say the least, it was the most original christening that I have ever attended. I have not since seen the Reverend Bill. I only hope he survived.

I woke on Monday the twenty-third somewhat refreshed and with the pleasant prospect of Angela ariving for the day. She was with me before ten of the clock and so began a lovely day. Nicola joined us for lunch at the Anchor Inn and it was all over too quickly. So little time and so much to talk about.

The hours fled by and I was waving her goodbye and hearing her promises to come again soon.

Those are my favourite days.

Sam has just joined me, begging for a little nourishment, so I shall leave you with the knowledge that I shall be thinking of you all doing your different things on Bank Holiday Monday as I sit quietly sipping my wine and nibbling a few peanuts.

Have fun and be careful.

Your as ever P.O.G.

* * *

6 September 1993

My Dear All,

Here I am again with the first week of September already in the past and the first signs of autumn with the odd early-morning nip in the air and the Virginia creeper beginning to turn to a burnt umber and brilliant red. The garden is beginning to look untidy and will need a brush-up within the next few weeks.

I noticed the children all wending their way schoolwards shepherded by their mums and carrying their packed lunches and overweight satchels. Actually they don't have satchels now, but great packs almost as large as the children themselves. The over-worked teachers will no doubt be sporting the suntans acquired in the Greek Islands during their well earned vacations and looking forward to half-term in a few weeks time. That is unless they take industrial action for an increase in salary to keep up with inflation. I am being unkind.

The Trade Union Conference is convening in Brighton with

all the Scots, Welsh or Irish leaders deciding what orders t
impart to the Labour Party and planning next year's sequence o
strikes.

I wonder who will be first? Arthur Scargill's Miners, Th
Transport and General Workers, The Electricians or one of th
many others. Do they draw lots for it? Perhaps the Bookmaker;
Union will give odds as to which.

'Phone you Duo now and win £100. Dial 081 3300 0033.'

I am still being unkind.

'UP THE WORKERS.'

I believe that I told you some time back that I had ne
neighbours who hailed from the Far East. I know very little mor
about them than I did then. They are very quiet and take thei
shoes off before going indoors in true Moslem fashion. The
leave them on the doorstep. The gentleman himself I now kno
is attending a course at the Military School of Electrical an
Mechanical Engineering at Bordon. Very rarely do they ope
any windows and it is quite obvious that gardening has ver
little appeal. Perhaps as their garden returns to jungl
conditions it will make them feel more at home.

I was surprised, when on answering a ring on my doorbell t
find a very small Asiatic lady standing at the door with a youn
infant in her arms. She, mostly by mime, indicated that sh
would like to use the phone. I invited her in and asked her if sh
was familiar with the dialling procedure. She was. Sh
produced a sheet of paper on which was written a number. I lef
her after telling her to ask me, if she had any difficulty. I retire
to the lounge so that she might make her call in private. I hear
her talking and it was obvious that she had made he
connection. I joined her as she replaced the receiver. The sma
child in her arms eyed me with considerable suspicion as if I wa
some sort of ogre. I asked her if she had finished and she did he
best to thank me although her English was somewha
minimal.

In an effort to be neighbourly I asked her where she cam
from and was surprised when she said, 'Borneo'.

That was the limit of our conversation and she was obviousl
only wishing to flee. I noticed by her figure as I opened the doo

116

for her, that it would not be long before she had another infant to nurse.

After she had gone I tried to remember what I knew about Borneo and the only vision that came to mind was a recollection from my schooldays. 'Head Hunters'. My geographic knowledge is sadly out of date. It was some time before the thought struck me and I hoped that she had not been making a phone call to her mum in some Far Eastern jungle. I have only had one fleeting glimpse of her since then. I am, however, becoming used to the odours of Oriental cooking which do not, I repeat, do not, make my mouth water. I have no urge to dash down to the Chinese Takeaway, and 'Far Flung Floyd' can remain in the far flung East as long as he likes.

Today I gained a suspicion that infant number two has arrived, but it is a mere suspicion arrived at from the fact that a small baby bath is visible in the kitchen window, a cradle has appeared on the patio and there is a variety of small clothing adorning the washing line. Perhaps more will come to light as time goes by. I am merely curious. I am not a racist although I do not want to be invited in for supper.

I did not attend the Family Eucharist yesterday but I am told that the television crew were there to film the service which included a baptism. Betty gave me details and said she posed for the cameraman. Apparently, the christening was a masterpiece of religious procedure.

They should have been there two weeks ago to film Oliver Mark! I reported that ceremony in my last letter. He would have won an Oscar.

Sister Hilda Margaret rang me a week ago to tell me that she had put her bungalow on the market, and was contemplating moving down to the town into a small flat overlooking the sea. She sounded very excited about the prospect.

Yesterday I rang her. She has got cold feet. I am not surprised. It would be a tremendous undertaking for an elderly lady rising eighty-eight. I think the cold feet will win. Anyway she told me to expect a visit from her within the next two weeks.

I am also expecting the bold Major of Tanks and his Rona on Friday or Saturday. I can't remember which.

117

Berty said over the phone that he would like to take me for lunch at the Anchor. I shall raise no objection.

Picture postcards are still arriving from all points of the compass with a preference for France. Susan and Phillip are soaking up the violet rays on the beaches of Le Cote D'Azur Richard and Nicola are probably touring vineyards sampling the various plonks and practising at becoming Europeople Roger and Hermione, after Devon, returned to Guernsey and hear on the grapevine that Roger has broken the New Year resolution that he made twenty-five years ago and has been seen swimming in the sea. John has been sailing the English Channel somewhere between Portsmouth and Cornwall. understand there were certain hiccups in the navigation. They were using a map of the motorways and nearly finished up on the M4. Taffy, I understand, has been motoring from port to port along the coast trying to find them to re-supply them with essentials (whiskey and gin), and Rachel joined the crew for several days but deserted before the difficult bit. John also tells me that he is perfecting his carpentry and joinery. He can now glue and screw things together so that they do not fall apart. He spends many hours adjusting plans to cope with the fact that he has sawn the wrong piece of wood in half and spends quite a lot of time sandpapering bloodstains. At least that knowledge solves his Christmas present. I shall give him a carpenter's first-aid kit. He also tells me that Her Majesty's Forces are surviving without him and that he and Taffy are off to Portugal for a short holiday next month.

I am still confirming my activities to a gentle daily meander up as far as the village church and back.

Now it is time I retired to the kitchen and prepared to replace my spent calories.

Be good. See you all sometime before Christmas.

Your increasingly ancient P.O.G.

*   *   *

118

26 September 1993

Dear All,

Good gracious, September nearly gone already and I don't know where. Time flies. Silly word, time.

Time has two complete pages to itself in the *Concise Oxford Dictionary*. One can waste time, which is probably what I am doing now. I hear people say they save time. Impossible. How can one save time? It is here and then it has gone. I will admit that the older one gets the quicker time seems to fly by but that is merely because old people have less time left. I am told that I am living on borrowed time. How can I borrow time? Do I have to repay it? There is 'day-time' and 'night-time'. When it is daytime I can sit in my armchair and drift into a refreshing sleep. At night time, when I go to bed, sleep evades me. I spend the time making endless cups of tea. I am disorientated. One can keep time, as in music.

Without the word 'time' we could not exist. We would be timeless.

Enough James. Stop. You are wasting time.

Actually the last weeks of September have had quite a few pleasant interludes. Firstly, Pauline came to tea with Holly and Chloe. Strawberry jelly. Jam tarts and chocolate rolls. The pitter-patter of tiny feet and shrill laughter. They grow up too quickly although Pauline would not agree with me there.

Next, for a fleeting stop on their holiday journey came the Royal Tank Regiment to take me out to lunch. Berty and Rona on their way to Folkestone. I am a lucky bloke.

A phone call from my old neighbours, Peter and Linda. Could they come and break their journey to Exeter and stay the night?

Yes, they would be very welcome. As they had not been able to attend my birthday party, I decided to indulge in a second one and booked a table for dinner at the Anchor. Betty joined us to make up the four and we had a hilarious evening meal – with no speeches.

Only a day passed before my dear sister Hilda Margaret arrived for the day. She was chauffered by her friends Ray and

119

Freda. This time it was Hilda who insisted on buying me another birthday lunch. Naturally we chose the Anchor. I shall soon have shares in it or at least I should get a commission. Hilda also presented me with the wall plates that were our mother's. For years I have longed to have them. A cherished memory of my boyhood days. Now they adorn my own wall. Mother always called them the 'Jack Sprat' plates although I do not know why. I rather feel that it was the first thing that came into her head when I asked her about them. Anyway for me they have always been the Jack Sprat plates.

And so September is slipping by with lovely autumn days and misty mornings, and all the shrubs decorated with hundreds of spiders' webs that glisten as the sun breaks through. Runner beans from the garden have been my favourite vegetable, and blackberries have formed the basis of my lunchtime sweets.

Now, what else has happened? Oh yes! The affair of Betty and the onions.

I think it was last Tuesday because that is the day when Betty does her weekly shop. I was in the kitchen washing up the pots and pans after lunch when I was surprised to see Betty flash by in the Flying Daffodil. I caught a momentary glimpse of her face. There was no shadow of doubt. Betty was angry. I could almost see the invective coming from her lips and there was a distinct blue haze around her.

Betty is very cross, I thought. Very angry indeed. An hour later I discovered the cause when she returned and came in, waking me from my afternoon nap.

Apparently, on returning home after finishing her shopping, she was puzzled by what she thought was an excessively large increase in prices which as we all know, do increase weekly. She decided to check the slip from the supermarket checkout.

She found that they had charged her twice for onions. Not only twice but the second charge was, wait for it, £8.59. She could not believe her eyes. £8.59 for five onions. Betty, being Betty, exploded and the old Flying Daffodil was steaming towards Alton with her foot through the floor. Vengeance quoth Betty. Death to all Gateway staff. If anything arouses Betty's ire it

120

is being cheated.

I leave you to visualise the scene in the supermarket when she confronted the staff with evidence of their wanton mistake. I believe that she had them all on the mat from the Manager downwards.

She received retribution. She was refunded with abject apologies together with compensation for the trouble they had caused her and her petrol used on a second journey.

It just goes to show how one can lose out in this computerised age. I wonder now how many times I have been overcharged. In future I shall watch out.

Other than that, life in Bentley changeth little. The rest of the country is in a spate of party political conferences and the threat of autumnal strikes is again in the news. Not *The Sun* newspaper; *The Sun* is still exploring the world of sex. This month they have covered the Michael Jackson affair of child abuse and housewives earning a bit on the side – quite lucratively too, if the reports are accurate. Wife swapping seems to be the latest thing. They will soon run out of ideas. Incidentally, I do not invest in *The Sun* newspaper. I occasionally browse through the one that Betty takes. She does not like me calling it a gutter paper. It is probably more amusing than *The Times* or *The Telegraph*.

The world news changes very little. The PLO leader, Mr 'Marrowfat' put a clean tea towel on his head and signed a treaty with Israel and promised to give up terrorism. The Bosnia Genocide War is no nearer a solution and Lord Owen is still negotiating peace. It keeps him from being redundant. The Americans are getting more deeply involved in Somaliland. Afghanistan is erupting again. The shooting match is still going on in Georgia. Moscow is in a turmoil and sanctions are being lifted from South Africa. All the other dozen or so wars are still simmering on.

And I am still wasting 'time'. It is time that I stopped waffling.

Till next time. Keep your fingers crossed so that there is a next time.

Your hopeful P.O.G.

* * *

14 October 1993

Dear All,

The BBC Weatherman, Mr Michael Haddock, states that it has been the wettest two weeks since Noah began building the Ark. Well I think he said since 1889 or thereabouts. Anyway it has certainly rained and is still doing so.

Apart from a day when Angela came up for a flying visit, I began to think that everyone had given me up for Epiphany or Pentecost of whatever season it is. But I was wrong. I had a letter from Hermione with the exciting news that Roger had been rejuvenated and is swimming in the sea again. I had heard that on the grapevine last month. He has also shaved off his beard and Hermione thinks that she has a new husband.

There was also a change of address card from Michael. They are back in South Petherton.

Last Sunday we celebrated Harvest Festival and sang *We plough the fields* and *All is safely gathered in*. Today on the news it seems that we were premature because the farmers are all pleading that they cannot get on to their fields to harvest their beet and potato crops and there will be a sugar and potato famine. Oh well! We can't be right all the time.

One other event has taken place. A voyage into history. My doorbell tinkled last Wednesday after lunch and there, on the doorstep, stood my old Troop Officer Major, the Hon. Peter Rous looking not a day older than when we last met in 1940. Admittedly, he was looking somewhat un-athletic and was propelling himself with a six-foot thumb stick. He is recovering from a fall and a fractured hip. We spent a wonderful two or three hours riding up and down the Khyber Pass again and digging forgotten names out of the past.

'Do you remember old Charlie Moyes?'

'Old fat Charlie? Of course I do. I remember when he . . . .'

'What happened to Paterson? Did he . . . ?'

We delved into regimental history and it was a splendid hour. We drank tea in military fashion; strong and sweet. None of this 'no sugar thank you'.

I did not want to let him go but drove him back to his daughter's at Broad Hatch with the video of the amalgamation of our regiment to the 17th Lancers. Perhaps we shall be able to return to bygone days again when he returns it.

I read something the other day that gave me food for thought. I can't remember what I was reading at the time but the author stated that: 'If a man cannot whistle it is a sign that he has homosexual tendencies.'

I became quite worried as it took me some considerable time before I managed it. Then I remembered that Maudie said that I was the only man who could whistle two hymn tunes at the same time.

So I am an ordinary homo. A man. Although the word homo, if I remember correctly, in Greek means 'wise'. That I most certainly am not or I would not be writing this rubbish.

Angela, bless her kind heart, has set me a project. I am to write a new book: 'P.O.G.'s Home Economy and Cook Book.'

More rubbish but it will give me 'food' for thought. That is not meant to be a pun.

Sam has a problem, Now that the autumn has arrived and winter is fast approaching, he is considering where he will make his winter quarters. He finds the garden swing seat subject to inclement weather so he is now testing out various indoor places of comfort. I do wish that he would make up his mind because this week he has commandeered the settee which is a nuisance when I have visitors. Last week he tried Maudie's bed. He thinks that he owns the place which I suppose really he does.

Now I really must stop this drivel. Perhaps something really interesting will crop up before the end of the month. Another war perhaps. Maybe a new prime minister.

So, just remember that I am still in the land of the living and remember me in your prayers if you say any.

As the Weatherman says,

Bye-bye for now,

As ever,

P.O.G.

123

* * *

Dear All,

The last two weeks of October have been pure autumn. After the early rains we have had picture-book frosty mornings and glorious sunny days. The trees are a blaze of russets and golds and the leaves are fluttering down making carpets for me to scuff through during my morning ambles.

Betty has been in making me feel quite ashamed watching her tidying up the garden, trimming back the shrubs, clearing the dead flowers from the beds and planting bulbs. She has even tucked Theresa Mona up for the winter and removed the dead geraniums from her grave, replanted daffodil bulbs for the spring and an array of mauve winter pansies to give a splash of colour during the late year days. She has even found time to go 'chestnutting' during her daily labours. She knows how I love fresh English chestnuts. I've also had wet walnuts from Mrs Grove and Filberts from the Country Market. It must be the squirrel in me. I love nuts.

I have also, during the last two weeks, had a personal MOT on my ageing bones. Someone told me that if I had not been seen by my doctor for three months, and I was found dead in my armchair or my bed, that there would have to be an autopsy. So I made an appointment to see Doctor Jonathan Moore. Very brave of me. The waiting room terrifies me. On this occasion I was surrounded by a bevy of ladies all suffering from a variety of ailments. My ears could not tell me what they were, even fully turned up. Female problems are beyond me anyway. It was with a great sense of relief when I heard my name called over the loudspeaker and I was able to present myself before Doctor Moore and explain to him the reason for my visit.

I like Doctor Moore. I have not seen him officially for three years. He checked my blood pressure, felt my pulse, shone a light and looked in my ears, and did in fact, do a thorough inspection. He came to a gratifying conclusion and pronounced that I was still alive. He told me to come back and see him next year.

124

I escaped without picking up any fatal germ from the occupants of the waiting room.

Later in the week, my old friend Major Peter Rous expressed a desire to see the audio people in Alton Hospital so I drove him down and had my own ears looked at and my hearing aids serviced at the same time.

Next on the agenda came my pedal extremities. My toenails were making holes in my socks. An SOS to my lady farrier, Miss Angela Spear, became necessary. She duly arrived and hacked away merrily, rectifying the fault. Why do my toenails grow so quickly? At £10 a visit they are becoming a liability. I shall need shoeing again before Christmas.

Only two items of body care left. My hair needed a short back and sides. I thought about doing my hair in a ponytail but Betty said that it would not suit me so a tinkle on the phone brought my Barber at the double. He plied his scissors and clippers and brought me up to date with village and world news. Mr Burningham is a fountain of knowledge. I now know things that went on in prisoner of war camps that I dare not disclose.

That leaves just my eyes. I have an appointment on Wednesday the third of November for a test to see if I can see. I feel confident that I can.

All that will bring me up to physical scratch. I have also bought a new pair of trousers, a pullover and a cravat.

So you will see that I have not been just idling my time away.

Keep away from winter germs. Gargle morning and night and don't forget to say your prayers.

As ever,

Your nonsensical P.O.G.

*   *   *

14 November 1993

Dear All,

Eureka! I can see. The Opthalmic Eye Lady shone lights into my eyes, made me read small print and declared that my

125

eyesight was even better than it was when she examined me last year. It took her all of six minutes and she only charged me £16, £8 an eye. Now that's what I call service.

I then developed a toothache. It was the £16 that brought it on. I took two aspirins and ignored it. Hey presto! The offending molar removed itself during my sleeping hours when I must have swallowed it. Anyway, I awoke one tooth less than I went to sleep with and no ache. The Dentist would have charged me £35 plus.

How's that for home economy?

The first two weeks of the month have disappeared. Guy Fawkes, gunpowder, treason and plot and lots of bangs frightened the life out of Sam on the fifth. The Houses of Parliament are still intact and the Chancellor of the Exchequer is preparing to increase our tax burden in the next two weeks. We need a new Guy Fawkes.

Did I tell you that Angela persuaded me to write a thesis on home economy and cooking for old age pensioners? She did and I have.

'P.O.G.'s Home Economy and Cook Book – A Must For Men Like Poor Old Grandad.'

It has turned out to be the biggest compilation of rubbish to date, although I must admit that I have been encouraged by the countless programmes and advertisements on this subject presented to me on the television. They are even worse than my own efforts.

I remember that in one of my 1992 letters I said the present generation was obsessed by sex. Sex is taking second place. Food dominates the media now.

But not English food!

Far Flung Floyd is conjuring up exotic dishes in eastern jungles. *A Cook's Tour of France:* lady named Mirielle Johnston is encouraging you all to catch the ferry and help the French eat something called *Salade Polletaise*. They are also offering her *French Cookery Course, Part Two* for only £12.99 plus £2.95 p & p. Antonio Carluccio: he will take you on a gastronomic tour of Southern Italy where he cooks a folded pizza for a religious ceremony. *Food and Drink:* learn how to cook venison and pheasant and other game and watch Jill Goolden swilling German wines around a glass, sniffing at their bouquet and drooling over them in ecstasy.

You can learn how the nation survived in the last war. Even the children's programme introduces the *Young Master Chef of the Year*. He displayed his skill with a Chinese stir fry which all the programme presenters sampled with chopsticks.

And it goes on. Even on radio. I myself still believe in the maxim: 'When in Rome do as the Romans do.'

If you want to eat French food go to France. If you want to eat Italian food go to Italy. Chinese in China and Indian in India. If you happen to be in Baghdad roll your sleeves up and dig into the communal mutton stew with the rest of them. If you are offered the 'sheep's eye' swallow it as you would an oyster and then belch heartily to show good manners.

I speak from experience. But, please, here in our dear old island why not eat English food – or Welsh, Scottish or Irish.

Why can't the English be English? Why can we not have a 'Cook's Tour of the British Isles'?

Here are a few ideas from some of our counties in alphabetical order:

> Bedfordshire: Catherine Cakes. So-called after Catherine of Aragon who used to live at Ampthill Castle. Special for the twenty-fifth of November, St Catherine's Day.
> Berkshire: Bacon Pudding and a dish called Poor Knights of Windsor.
> Buckinghamshire: Aylesbury Cherry Bumpers and Stokenchurch Pie.
> Cambridgeshire: Ely Milk Cheese. Cambridge Sauce.
> Cheshire: Chester Pork Pie. Flummery and Chester Pudding.
> Cornwall: Cornish Pasties. Figgie Hobbin and Kidley Broth.
> Cumberland: Clipping-time Pudding, Burnet Wine and Cumberland Rum Butter.
> Derbyshire: Bakewell Tarts. Medley Pie and

127

Chesterfield Rabbit Stew.

And so on and so on. I could take you on a real 'Cook's Tour' with specialities in every one of our lovely counties. If you would like the recipes send an SAE and £100.99 plus 25p p & p to P.O.G. and you will be very lucky to get any satisfaction. You just might.

It's amazing how I ramble on. I am probably going a little bonkers. It is probably caused by all this home economy and the thought of all the ironing that needs to be done. I shall go and pour myself a flagon of English bitter.

On second thoughts perhaps I should dash down to Macdonalds and get myself a beefburger and a Diet Coke.

Perhaps I should go even more British and try the Chinese Cuisine Eating House in Farnham. Someone said they even have geishas but I think they were pulling my leg.

What about a Hampshire Friar's omelette? No, that would take too long. I'll stick to my first idea and just have a beer.

Be good now and don't lose your chopsticks.

Your own ancient chef P.O.G.

*   *   *

30 November 1993

Dear All,

The last two weeks of the month have been somewhat traumatic. I lave learnt a lesson. Never, I repeat, never joke about toothache. My flippant boasting about the tooth that I swallowed was a ghastly mistake.

On the evening of Friday the twentieth another tooth erupted and an agonising pain began to throb around my aged gums. Ah! I thought, I will take a couple of aspirins, go to sleep and it will remove itself during the night. Did it? No it did not. It yelled 'Revenge' and really took off. I spent the next twelve hours in agony desperately trying to dispel the stabbing pain with aspirins and gallons of hot tea. By dawn I was only semi-conscious. Why do these things always happen at weekends?

128

In desperation I sent an SOS to Susan. Find me a dentist, I pleaded. With her usual efficiency Susan said, 'Leave it to me, James. I'll call you back.'

I took two more aspirins and waited. The pain subsided. I nearly rang her to abort the operation but she beat me to it.

'Ten twenty, James. A dentist in Alton. Alderney House. I'll pick you up just before ten, O.K?'

I was committed. Be brave James. Put on your famous fearless expression. There's nothing to it. I lie. I was terrified. Why does the Dentist's chair always arouse such visions of the torture chamber?

And before I knew it I was flat on my back in a reclining chair and a white-coated gentleman named Mr Collins was jabbing needles into my gum. Within thirty minutes I was safely back at No. 17 Eggars Field minus one more tooth and a numbness pervading my mouth and lips. I gradually recovered a sense of feeling and was again in the land of the living.

By teatime I was more or less back to normal and Richard, with the good Nicola, appeared to cheer me up. Susan too returned to see if I had recovered. How lucky I am to have help at my fingertips.

And now with my 'choppers'safely depleted I am consigned to a diet of soups and porridge!

What price my wasted efforts writing a cook book?

So much for my physical condition.

The weather has really got into its winter stride with hard frosts so that I have only ventured out when absolutely necessary. Pauline came and took me out to the Forest Lodge Garden Centre which is now a riot of Christmas decorations with Father Christmases on skis, nodding reindeer, coloured lights and all the usual seasonal delights. Chloe and a young man named Joshua, whom I met for the first time, kept Pauline busy rescuing cuddly teddy bears, dinosaurs, rabbits and every other conceivable toy animal from their eager hands. I had forgotten the speed with which three-year-old children delve into everything.

Anyway, it was fun for me even if it was a little harassing for Pauline.

Now on this last day the Chancellor of the Exchequer has had his big moment. Another effort to get the country out of the 'red'. At least I know now that we have at last paid for the cannon balls that were used at the Battle of Waterloo! Now only a mere fifty billion pounds on the debit side to deal with. Chicken feed!

His whole speech was a 'con' from start to finish. It was an illusion. All done with mirrors. There should at least be a saving in Westminster fuel bills. The 'hot air' that rises ought to keep them warm for months.

VAT on that lot could write off the national debt. It will no doubt give the Opposition plenty to rant off about and earn their meagre salaries and generate a lot more 'hot air'.

I shall pay up and do my duty in helping to boost the Economy. I have no choice anyway. Cheer up James.

Christmas is coming and the geese are getting fat. My hat will be on the hall table for your pennies when next you call.

The last Saturday in November 1993 will at least go down in history.

Against all the odds England beat the All Blacks! And what a match it was. I'm sure that many thousands of English fingernails were gnawed down to the elbows. I even felt that the ever increasing cost of the TV licence was justified. Until Sunday anyway.

And now tomorrow will see me into December, so I must be thankful for small mercies and grateful that I am still with you and only two teeth less than I had in October.

Keep well and don't forget to gargle. I am on a daily dose of cod-liver oil in an effort to lubricate some of my more obstinate joints. I find it much easier to lubricate my throat.

As always,

Your P.O.G.

* * *

Dear All,

I was under the impression that the holiday time of the year was over. Wrong again James. Heather Rudin sent me a card from China. She is travelling the ancient Silk Road to Peking and from the brief descriptions is now head over heels in love with the Chinese. My own knowledge is limited to the stories that I read in my youth of the Boxer Rebellion, Fu Man Chu and Anna May Wong. And MMS *Amethyst* running the gauntlet down to the River Yantze. No doubt I shall hear more on Heather's return and certainly China will be in the news as Chris Patten struggles to insist on democracy for Hong Kong when the lease expires in 1996. I scent another load of political mayhem and upheaval when the 'Yellow Peril' takes over.

A second card from Gibraltar. Georgia is enjoying the fleshpots of a luxury cruise in the good ship *Sea Princess*, 714 passengers and 400 crew. Eight passenger decks, three lounges with dance floors, four bars, theatre, library, casino, shop, cardroom, hairdressing and beauty salon, three swimming pools (one heated with jacuzzi), sauna, gym and adjacent massage rooms.

How's that for living it up? After Gib it is Greece, Turkey, Egypt, Jordan, Israel and back. And all she has got to do, I am told, is entertain the 714 passengers by giving recitals on her panpipes. I only hope that she does not get left on Mount Olympus when they reach Greece.

Now it is the run up to Christmas. The mad rush will gather momentum as the days fly by.

There are also birthdays. Birthdays in December are unfair on the celebrants who are lucky to get any presents at all.

I am seriously thinking of lobbying my MP to propose an Act of Parliament placing a ban on cohabitation and sexual intercourse during the month of March and the first two weeks of April which would restrict the amount of births in December. People should be encouraged to control those hormones that go rampaging about during the spring. My doctor says that I am a 'spoilsport' and that it would not be a popular legislation. I can only try. The only birthday that I would accept is Jesus on the twenty-fifth.

Katharine, when she was around eleven years old and staying with Granny and me at Crocketts thought that when we went to church to sing carols we should also sing:

Happy Birthday to You, Happy Birthday to You,
Happy Birthday dear Jesus, Happy Birthday to
You.

Why not? I must ask the Reverend Bill for his opinion.

I have been to see Doctor Moore again to have my head looked at. He gave me a local anaesthetic and removed an unsightly lump from my left temple. I am handsome once more.

Betty came in at lunchtime today suffering from a raging toothache. She thinks that she caught it from me. Anyway I phoned the Dentist and whisked her into Alton. She was not as lucky as me. Her tooth was stubborn. It was also more expensive. It cost her £25 whereas mine was removed for a mere £15. We have decided that the dentists now charge £1 per minute. The removal of mine only took fifteen minutes but hers ran on to twenty-five minutes. It is something to do with inflation. She also has to have adjustments made to her dentures which rockets the price up into three figures.

I am going to survive on porridge and soup. I shall not clutter my mouth up with a load of homemade choppers.

Actually I remember now that Richard put spares in my Octogenarian Survival Kit on my birthday. I must dig them out. This Welfare State gets more expensive daily.

Now I really must get down to thinking about Christmas. All those cards to write. I bet my address book is out of date and everyone will have moved to new locations. Then I have to phone around to find out where they all are.

It is such a great strain on my mental and physical powers. I get all stuck up with sellotape and I am always losing the scissors. I think that I am approaching the age when I shall plead incapacity. I've pickled onions and beetroot. I suppose I shall

132

have to make mince pies and Sam will insist on me decorating the tree so that he can amuse himself removing the tinsel and ornamentations.

Now I shall go and find a reviving libation and do some mental preparation.

If this happens to be the last letter of P.O.G. for 1993 I had better wish you all a Merry and Happy Christmas now.

Perhaps I shall see some of you before the end of the year.

I lift my glass. Your very good health one and all.

Remember. Don't drink and drive.

God Bless you all,

P.O.G.

* * *

Christmas 1993

Dear Holly,

This story is especially for you. It is called:

The Little Girl That Father Christmas Forgot

Amanda Jane lived with her mummy and daddy in a tiny house in a little lane on the edge of the village. It was very dificult to find unless you knew exactly where it was.

They were very poor and her daddy could not find work so that there was very little money to buy anything except food and clothes to keep them warm.

It was Christmas, and Amanda had written a little letter to Father Christmas asking him to bring her anything that he could spare from his store and on Christmas Eve she hopefully hung up one of her very small stockings.

It was barely light when she awoke on Christmas morning and the first thing she did was to look at her

133

stocking to see if he had been.

It was empty. Just as she had left it. He had forgotten her. The tears welled up in her eyes. It wasn't fair. Why had he forgotten her?

She knelt on her bed and looked sadly out of the window at the cold, bleak winter morning. It had been snowing again and everything was still and silent.

Then, looking out into the lane she saw a great sledge with reindeer harnessed to it. A red-robed gentleman with a flowing white beard was preparing to get into the driver's seat. It was Father Christmas. He was throwing what seemed to be an empty sack into the back of the sledge.

Amanda, without even stopping to put on slippers or a dressing gown flew down the stairs and out into the lane running as fast as she could and crying out, 'Father Christmas, Father Christmas, wait for me.'

She ran up to the sledge and breathlessly looked up into his surprised eyes.

'Father Christmas,' she cried, 'you have forgotten me. My stocking is empty.'

The old gentleman picked her up in his arms as surprised as she was.

'Forgotten you my dear? How on earth could I do such a thing?' He picked up the sack from the back of the sledge and felt around it. 'There is nothing left. It is empty. That is strange. It's not like me to forget anyone.'

He felt again. 'Wait a minute, there's something here.'

He turned his sack inside out and out fell a little parcel. It was a very, very small spinning top.

'Ah! That's it. One of my magic spinning tops. Is your name Amanda Jane? This was meant for you. It is very special and if you look after it, it will bring you lots and lots of luck. When you spin it, it will light up and play a little tune all the time it is spinning. How could I forget to leave it for you? What a good job you caught me just in time. Now I must fly. I have a long way to go.'

He gave her a quick hug and a kiss and as she grasped the little top in her hand she saw him pick up the reins and wave as he drove off. She watched him disappear into the distance before she ran back indoors.

In her bedroom she examined the little top. It was bright blue with little stars painted on its rim. She held it between her forefinger and thumb and tried to spin it. She tried and tried before she got the knack.

As it spun it lit up, lights flashed from it and a magical little tune which sounded like, 'Happy Birthday to You, Happy Birthday to You'.

Well it was the birthday of Jesus so perhaps that was why it was so magical.

Amanda could not stop spinning it. Naturally her mummy and daddy had to have a go as well.

And do you know that from that day onwards everything seemed to get better. Her daddy found work and all their worries disappeared.

The little magic top really did work magic.

Amanda never saw Father Christmas again but she treasured the little top more than anything else and even now that she has grown up it is still secure in the drawer of her dressing table and she still sometimes spins it and it still flashes lights and plays the same little tune.

'Happy Christmas to you' or is it 'Happy Birthday'?

Now the little top has turned up again so perhaps you will look after it and it will bring lots and lots of luck to you as well.

Lots and lots of love from,

P.O.G.

* * *

THE LETTERS OF P.O.G
1994

Dear All,

Nineteen ninety four! I've made it. Hooray! At one stage I had my doubts. And now another Christmas has disappeared into history and tomorrow being the twelfth night I must take down all the decorations.

Where did Christmas go? I seemed to spend days selecting, buying and doing up presents, writing cards, making mince pies and boiling ham. The Postman remarked that I had some strange people living in my house as he delivered letters addressed to: 'Mr Samson Cat', 'P.O.G.', 'Old James', 'Betty c/o', 'Captain J F' and the odd 'Mr J F'.

The Mr J Fs were two £50 Ernies which gave me great pleasure Betty says that where there are two there is always a third. It has not yet materialised!

On Christmas Eve John collected me and delivered me into the hands of the Horse People at Tollard where for two days I was feasted and wined with Katie and Lulu preparing and presenting the Christmas Day meal in a truly professional fashion that could not have been bettered by Delia Smith. The whole morning was spent sitting under the Christmas tree surrounded by five semi-wild Jack Russells, old Pee the Border Collie, and Debussy and Jaque the two cats. We undid present after present while David sat patiently disposing mountains of wrapping paper into a great black plastic sack. We ate nuts and chocolates washed down with mulled wine.

On waking up Christmas morn I looked out onto a vista of snow-covered landscape. A White Christmas. It was a wonderful picture but I was thankful that I did not have to venture out to water and feed fifty or so horses as did the others. They came in full of excitement saying how beautiful it was. I know now that I am getting very old.

Christmas left me with only one regret. I was assuaged with a feeling of guilt. I heard no carols and I did not go to church to say Happy Birthday to the reason for it all. I was given the opportunity and could have attended the Midnight Service with Angela's neighbour but I turned it down saying that I was too tired and too old. What a feeble excuse. Even Amanda our old Christmas fairy with whom Angela had decorated my bedroom door seemed sad. She did not look happy. I must ask Angela to bring her back home where she really belongs with her old friends on my tree.

I wonder how many of you made the same excuse? Too busy! Too tired! Or just not bothered. It is going to be my No. 1 New Year resolution. If I am given the grace to survive for another Christmas I shall not let Him down again.

On Sunday the twenty-sixth it was Angela's turn to feed us all and after another fabulous lunch they all played Cluedo. My powers of deduction were dulled by over eating and drinking so that I lapsed into a sleepy coma.

Monday the twenty-seventh was Boxing Day and the equestrian element were back in the saddle. In fact Angela was saddling up before I had opened my weary eyes. It was Katie's day off and as I could not be of any use she drove me back home to Bentley. We stopped off at the Anchor Inn for a quick lunch before she returned. Sam was pleased to see me although he pretended to ignore me. Betty had kept the home fires burning and came in to help me undo all the presents that I had left behind. At this stage I must say 'Thank you' one and all. I had bottles of port, rum, Rumkoff; a wine rack; socks (one pair were decorated with a picture of Rudolf the Red Nosed Reindeer); Liquorish Allsorts; chocolates; books (one was *The Guiness Book of Military Blunders* which strange to say has no mention of Captain James F who was without a doubt the greatest blunder of all time); a wonderful white Paisley woollen scarf which I wore to church on Sunday. I had a pink stocking filled with goodies that included an amazing pair of spectacles and a monocle together with nuts and oranges. I also had a wonderful footstool, hand made by the new Cabinet Maker in the family. Thank you John.

Please all of you accept this as my thank you letter and keep your fingers crossed ready for next time.

New Years Eve arrived. I drove into Farnham and visited the new Sainsbury Superstore. I purchased two fresh lobsters and invited Betty to join me for supper. Lobster salad followed by

Rumkopf and vanilla blancmange. We washed it down with a bottle of Hock. We toasted 1994 with a glass of port as Bong Bing chimed the midnight hour and croaked a feeble *Auld Lang Syne* as we started into another year.

Since then I have been trying to search my memory for something that I achieved in 1993 and have reached the conclusion that I achieved nothing other than that I am still here. I saw the death of my regiment, lived through the Recession and I am told that the country is now on the verge of recovery. The world overall is still in a mess and I see little news but a multitude of politicians sitting round tables of peace while little wars flare up all over. I see the latest conflict is now in Mexico.

I am making no new resolutions other than the one I mentioned earlier. I shall still continue my search for a publisher. I shall still write more rubbish, pray for you all and hope for the best.

Now I shall just wish you all a very, very Happy and Prosperous 1994 and trust that you will spare a few moments to think of

Your optimistic P.O.G.

*   *   *

30 January 1994

Dear All,

I wrote my last letter just as the New Year commenced and since then I have experienced snow, ice and a blackout in which I reverted to candles and camping Gaz. It is amazing but the smallest sign of a blizzard always brings a power failure. Since the snow we have had incessant rain which has caused havoc in parts of the South. Poor old Chichester probably had it worst of all. We in good old Bentley suffered not apart from the hazards of venturing out which I did not do. Hibernate James, I said.

I did have a visit from my 'fan club'. Pauline brought Holly and Chloe to cheer me up. A fan club with two members is better than none at all. Both Katharine and Susan paid me visits

141

to thank me for birthday gifts and I have had letters from the rest of the clan.

The national news has started with parliamentary scandals with a fresh batch of MPs involved in extra sexual activities. I am beginning to wonder if it is organised by the females themselves so that they can flog their stories to the more dubious newspapers and retire on the proceeds.

Westminster Borough Council is also in the news with allegations of fiddle. A mere twenty-one point something million pounds of tax payers' money seems to have been squandered somethere. Well it will keep the Press going for some considerable time. Let's have another enquiry.

Peace talks from Brussels to Moscow are thriving with apparently little success although from the smiles and handshaking by the negotiators I could be wrong. Ireland is anyone's guess. The IRA are still enjoying throwing their bombs and sniping the odd soldier.

Mr 'Marrowfat' has put on a clean tea towel in the hope that the PLO will listen to him.

So it seems that little has changed.

Now. You are not going to believe this! The other night I awoke around 1 a.m. with the smell of cooking pervading my bedroom. I immediately thought that I had left the cooker on and with one eye open I descended the stairs to investigate. I had not. Then I realised that it was not an English odour. It was my Asian neighbours having a midnight nosh. It is quite amazing how this smell of cooking can invade me. It just filters through the window frames, down the chimney and probably through the walls. Apart from wearing a gas mask there is little I can do to prevent it. It seems to be more noticeable when the wind is strong from the northwest.

I thought it strange that they could be enjoying nocturnal feasts but went back to sleep.

It struck me that it was even more strange when it happened the following night and yet again the night after.

Then the reason dawned on me.

Ramadan! You must all know what Ramadan is. The ninth month of the Moslem year. The season of fasting when Moslems

142

may not eat between dawn and sunset. Originally it was one of hot months but now passing through all seasons by lunar reckoning. My trouble is that I have no idea how long it will last. Being awakened by the smell of barbecued sheeps' eyes and Oriental odours in the small hours of the night is a little much.

However, I must be kind and patient. At least I never hear them or see them for that matter and I can put up with a few odd smells and perhaps the wind will change and blow from the South.

Of course I would be wrong. It may not be Ramadan. Perhaps they have decided that they like eating at night.

Time will tell.

And now January is bringing this first month of 1994 to a close. It has been a violent four weeks. Weatherwise we have had everything from Arctic to sub-Tropical weather and in the rest of the world, a massive Earthquake in San Francisco and terrible forest fires in Sydney. We, in this green and pleasant land, apart from poor old Chichester, have been fortunate. I have even managed two complete circuits of the village while the sun shone.

Semi-hibernation has enabled me to steer clear of the flu-ridden masses and all I have suffered was a runny nose. I have avoided all females who have a tendency to plant kisses on one and imbibed my daily hot rum – and on occasions, nightly as well. Rum I find is the cure for all evils.

Either the wind has changed direction or 'Ramadan' is over. The nocturnal feasting seems to have ended. So now I must prepare to face February. I wonder what it has in store for me. The BBC is currently deep in what is known as the 'Year of the Family'. I have already written the Editor of the *Radio Times* about all the codswallop written and spoken about it.

I shall give you my views in my first February letter. Be patient and love one another.

I am still with you – just. Now I must away and mix my 'Elixir of Life'.

As ever in love, hope and charity,
Your ancient P.O.G.

* * *

Dear All,

Sunday the sixth of February. Angela's birthday. Fifty-six years ago I was riding a horse across the maidan around the city of Secunderabad in the Province of the Nizam of Hyderabad unaware that my daughter had arrived in this world of ours.

It was four long weeks before I received a letter telling me of this momentous occasion in my life. Today I would have known at the press of a button. I could have had a photograph via a fax machine. In a few hours I could have flown home and been at the bedside.

Do we really appreciate this conquest of time and space? Are we better people for all this advance in technology? I sometimes wonder.

I did say in my letter that I would give you my views on the 'Year of the Family' but I have changed my mind. Thinking about it I come to the conclusion that families have not changed since the year dot. One has good families and bad families. We are fairly lucky. I think we can say that we are among the good. Do you agree? I expect that you sometimes have a few arguments but I don't think that you come to blows and I hope that you do not use profane language. Ha! Ha! Maudie and I had a few notable battles which I somehow seemed to lose. I always used the 'count ten' method and said 'Oh! Bother!' instead of ****. I always let Maudie think that she had won and surrendered gracefully, gently waving my white flag, and pouring her a gin and tonic. It takes a few years to learn the technique but once you've learnt it life becomes quite pleasant.

With our Prime Minister urging us to get 'back to basics', whatever that means, and politicians sleeping with their secretaries during the week and hardly ever going home, I feel that their 'Year of the Family' is somewhat onerous. The 'Royal' example is not really any encouragement either.

So, yet again, I leave it all to you.

144

Anyway the sun is shining. The churchyard is a carpet of snowdrops and the spring bulbs are springing everywhere. The birds are singing and I am slowly emerging from any hibernation.

Betty is still confounding me with wise superstitious forecasts. I dropped a spoon the other day and she immediately said that I should receive a visitor. Richard and Nicola arrived to prove her right. Then a day or so later I let a knife slip from my fingers. She said that I was due for a disappointment. I am expecting rejections from publishers any day now. I asked her what would happen if I dropped a fork.

'Oh, you'll just have to pick it up,' she replied.

John Mortimer says, and I quote,

> 'You don't mellow as you get older, you become more extreme. You have nothing to lose and so don't give a damn what you say.'

But is there a secret to life? 'The secret of everything is to make people laugh.'

I do try. I have just written the 'Sermon of the Month' and given it to the Reverend Bill but I doubt that he will use it. Actually I pinched it from a book of cat stories that I was given for Christmas. It may amuse you.

SERMON OF THE MONTH.

This is the story of a ship's cat. He was a very healthy and beautiful tabby cat. The Captain of the ship was very fond of his cat and he was also a very religious man.

Each Sunday as the ship sailed its way across the oceans the Captain would hold a church parade on the poop deck for the entire crew. The ship's cat never failed to attend and it became very devout and enjoyed the vigorous hymn singing. He became known as 'The Holy Terror' and the undisputed king of any port at which they dropped anchor.

Then it happened one day when the Captain went ashore that he fell into the clutches of a female 'Nonbeliever' and he married her. She bewitched him and persuaded him that he was wasting his time with his Sunday devotions. So they were stopped.

The ship rapidly changed from a happy ship to one on which all the crew became dismal and sad and the 'Holy Terror' went into a decline. His coat lost its lustre and he became daily thinner and thinner.

The First Mate became worried. He worried about the crew who became lax and careless and he worried about the ship's cat.

It was the fault of the Captain's new wife and both the Mate and the cat knew that the Captain should never have married, as they termed her, an 'Angrynostic'.

Things got worse and the situation desperate. The crew became lethargic and careless about their duties and the 'Holy Terror' was at 'death's door'. The Mate pleaded with the Captain to re-institute the Sunday Church Parade and so save the cat's life and invest the crew with their former vigour.

The Captain, in his 'heart of hearts' had also missed his Sunday worship and was very upset to see his cat and crew in such a sorry state. So, defying his 'Angrynostic' wife he ordered the Mate to parade the crew on the following Sunday.

From that day on the ship became once again a happy ship and the 'Holy Terror' regained his former robust health and spread the 'Good News' at every port at which the ship dropped anchor.

So, the 'Angrynostic' was defeated. She was also converted and whenever she sailed with them joined in the hymn singing and worship. There is a moral somewhere in this story so let us remember the 'Holy Terror', sing our hymns and pray for all 'Angrynostics'.

So with these thoughts I leave you to prepare for Saint Valentine's Day and Pancake Tuesday.

Love one another and don't forget the lemon.

As ever,

Your P.O.G.

* * *

20 February 1994

Dear All,

The last day of February. For some unknown reason a cloud of gloom has descended on me and I have not been my usual happy little soul. The reason for this phenomenon is probably due to a number of reasons. Firstly the news which tells me that the world is in a very sorry state but I expect that you are as fully aware of that as I am. Secondly the weather which has not been able to remain constant for more than twenty-four hours at a time and one has never known what to expect until the curtains are drawn each morning. It has varied daily and my old barometer has gone completely crazy. Thirdly my ageing bones have become more aged and if you really would like to know the state of my physical condition I suggest that you come and listen to Betty's chiming clock as it strikes the noon-day hour. I feel exactly like her clock.

And now it is Lent which is always a somewhat sad time although I doubt whether many in this Christian land know what it is all about. The ladies in the village are holding their weekly Lenten lunches or as I know them 'Holy Soups'. I attended one last year but as I was the only male penitent I have been rather wary of them since.

I have also become aware of the insidious way in which the female element of our country is gradually moving in to all the former male dominated professions. Every time that I switch on my television I am confronted by a new face. The News, sport programmes, sit-coms such as *Birds of a Feather*, whose husbands are intelligent enough to remain in prison, *Absolutely Fabulous*, a dreadful show. The ladies are replacing Taggart and Inspector

Morse in the detection of crime (probably a good thing in respect of Taggart), in fact in every little corner of our existence. They will soon be competing for the top jobs in the Church. I could go on.

I remember that some years ago the Two Ronnies did a show named *The Worm Turns* in which the country was completely run by the ladies. I think the writer of that show was distinctly prophetic.

Perhaps it might not be such a bad thing. Men will become surplus to the establishment and just a few kept in stud farms around the country.

A few bright moments have enlivened my days. Angela came to cheer me up. Pauline brought my fan-club for jelly and doughnuts and my old friend Ken Peet brought his 98-year-old mum for a fleeting visit. We had not seen one another for thirty years. Richard and Nicola joined us for the day and it was a very happy reunion. Ken's mother was amazing. I expected her to get out her skipping rope but she had left it at home. Just another example of feminine stamina. Ninety-eight and still enjoying life.

We males have no chance. Now I must stop. Forgive a dreary note of gloom. Perhaps March will see a revival in my condition.

Be good now and pray for a return to health for Betty's clock.

As ever,

Your decrepit P.O.G.

P.S.

For Hilda Margaret:

I have just come across John's baptismal card and I notice that you are his godmother. I had forgotten but I do hope that you have ensured that he has grown up to live a godly and Christian life!

I trust that you have also remembered him in your will.

*   *   *

Dear All,

Another month is on the verge of flitting into history. It has not left me brimming over with *joie de vivre.* Fleeting visits from Angela and John lifted me from the slough of despair for a few brief hours and one or two sunny days allowed me to potter or should I say stagger around the village. Spring came on the twenty-first and my big sister, now four feet four inches tall and weighing five stone, celebrated her eighty-eighth birthday.

Hilda Margaret is proof that the ladies are more resilient than we poor males. In fact March has seen the resurgence of the female sex. They have been gathering momentum in strength every day. Mrs Pankhurst would be proud of you girls. No longer is it necessary for you to throw yourselves in the path of the Derby runners or tie yourselves to railings protesting about the evil male. You are winning hand over fist.

This March of 1994 brought a massive rise in the sale of Mother's Day cards, chocolates and flowers. Women priests were ordained in the Church of England and are now on the bottom rung of the ladder to the bishoprics. I wonder who will be the first to take up residence in Lambeth Palace. The first all-woman radio station went on the air and women newsreaders, sport commentators, chat show presenters, stand-up comics, human rights, social problems and weather forecasters increase in number daily. There is no shadow of doubt, the girls are gradually taking over. It will soon be the boys who will be complaining of sex discrimination. I for one have no desire to throw myself in the path of the Grand National field, chain myself to railings or parade outside No. 10 Downing Street carrying a banner saying, 'THE P.M. IS UNFAIR TO JAMES'

I am all for handing over the reins and letting the girls have a go. Anyway I'm past it now.

Tomorrow I shall have reached another milestone in this transitory life and for the first time in around sixty years, give or take a year or so, I shall be without wheels. And that does not include my youthful days when I had a bicycle and motorcycles.

'TVJ 569 S' has reached the age where it can no longer pass it
mechanical medical and I am having it retired to the automobil
cemetery. It will be a sad day and if you see me wearing a blacl
tie you will know why.

I have an appointment to see my medical advisor at 11 a.m.
feel that I too will fail the test. The important bits are wearing ou
fast.

Samson is a picture of health apart from his ears. He seems to
lose a little more fur each time he goes out. Betty came in to
Farnham with me last week to see my financial advisor and
establish a pension fund for Mr Samson Cat. He still needs
Whiskers when I'm not here to provide them.

I must leave you now and wend my way to the Doctor. I shal
probably sit in the surgery until noon and inhale a few deadly
germs. As I said, like Betty's chiming clock I am wearing ou
more each day.

Be good and remember your,

Ailing P.O.G.

P.S.

The Doctor told me that I am still alive so I suppose I mus
take her word for it. Yes, even my doctor is a lady. In fact my
appointment for eleven got me in to see her at noon. I was the
only male patient. You see. All women.

* * *

29 April 1994

Dear All,

Incredible though it may seem April started on the first. All
Fool's Day. Samson's fifth birthday. He enjoyed a feast of fresh
pig's liver washed down with the cream from the top of the milk
and then went to sleep for the remainder of the day.

It also happened to be Good Friday so I started the day with
hot cross buns for breakfast and then spent the rest of the day
quietly meditating. That was because I was not feeling my usual
healthy vigorous self. Something had started to go wrong with

150

my inside mechanism and I had been forced to seek the advice of my doctor the day previously. If one begins to feel unwell it always seems to happen on weekends or national holidays. Doctor Way was kindness itself and convinced me that I should not die before Easter had passed. Anyway, I spent Easter weekend with what I can only describe as a nasty 'guts ache'. However, I did put on my best face and convinced myself, nearly, that there was nothing wrong with me.

On Saturday Pauline popped in with Holly and Chloe to cheer me up. I was presented with a chocolate frog and in return I hid a quantity of smallish chocolate eggs around the house for the little ones to play hunt the eggs with. Children must have a nose for chocolate eggs for in no time at all they had discovered at least four each and lost no time in commencing to dispose of them. Holly was on her fourth egg when Pauline, reading one of the silver paper wrappings, asked me if I knew that they were liqueur chocolate eggs. I did not. I had no idea that they made such eggs. However, by this time Holly had disposed of two which were said to be whiskey, one brandy and the fourth a Cointreau filled egg. Chloe was only one egg behind her. We could see no visible effects and no signs of inebriation so we concluded that the eggs contained mere token flavours. Anyway it all added to the gaiety.

I had a second egg from Susan who came over later in the day.

Easter Sunday I spent feeling a little sorry for myself and somewhat uncomfortable inside. Betty went to church and did my praying for me and raised her voice with the 'Alleluias'.

So taking things all round it was not an Easter that I enjoyed. Nicola and Georgia came over for tea on one day leaving Richard at home to sleep off excessive golf. I can't remember which day that was.

Easter over, I was back to see Doctor Way with my inside showing little signs of normality. I am now waiting for an appointment with a 'bellyologist'. The medical title eludes me.

'Theresa versus James 569 Squire' has gone for disposal. It seems strange to be without wheels. Betty gave me a lift into

Alton in the Flying Daffodil so that I might replenish my larder and get Sam some Whiskers.

The weather had reverted to ice and snow although on Monday the eleventh we had a heat wave and I managed a complete circuit of the village.

I began to think that the rain would never cease and after the disastrous abortive start to the Grand National in 1993 it seemed likely that the water-logged course would result in a cancellation this year. It was touch and go until the last minute before the thumbs up was given. The race started smoothly without any trouble but the soft ground proved too much for most of the runners and out of thirty-six starters only six horses completed the course with Richard Dunwoody just managing to keep his horse with its nose in front. Miineehoma ran a superb race. What stupid names they give horses these days. The other highlight for me was Mrs Rosemary Henderson who rode a magnificent race to become the first lady of Aintree with fifth place on her Fiddlers Pike.

I regret to say that the Grand National was the only television that April has so far produced that justified any viewing. It made me feel that the licence fee is worth continuing. I would also miss *Postman Pat* and *Fireman Sam* but little else.

I am pleased to report that my beloved TVJ 569 S is going to Farnham Technical College to be used for student instruction and I feel happier knowing that it may do something towards instructing our future road users and mechanics.

There will now be a slight pause in this epistle so that I may see what the last weeks of April will bring.

And here I am now in the last week of April. It has been, and still is, an uncomfortable few weeks with my insides in a turmoil. Today, however, I feel that there are signs of improvement. This upsurge in physical well-being has probably been caused by my weekend visitor. My dear old friend Ken Peet rang to ask if he could have a bed for the night of Saturday and duly arrived just after lunch. It was good to see him although he is in a rather sorry state. The spine that he fractured many years ago has erupted into a major problem for which he is only given a fifty–fifty chance of overcoming. At least it made me think that my own belly ache was hardly worth a mention. However, I was pleased to see him and we had a great few hours together and sat over one of my better culinary efforts back over the years. He had to leave just after breakfast on Sunday to return home and look after his 98-year-old mum.

Sam was somewhat annoyed to have his bed occupied by a stranger and spent the night on the lavatory seat in a sulk. Ken's early departure at least got me up in time to attend church with Betty doing chauffeuse in the Flying Daffodil.

And now on this Monday morning the sun is shining. My washing is almost ready to hang out on the line and I am feeling more human.

I did have a nightmare. I think it was last Wednesday. I don't know what it was all about but I was involved in a frightful battle and my bedside light went flying, my bedside alarm clock finished up under the dressing table but the glass of water beside it remained untouched. I think that I must have won because I was not wounded and only suffered a broken electric light bulb.

This week sees the last of a heavy birthday month; just Katie Roberts and Hermione left for the last two days.

I will leave this open now just in case the last few days produce anything worth recording. Who knows? Something really exciting may happen.

It hasn't. At least we have had three lovely days and I was even able to sit on the swingseat in the sun and watch my garden grow. And for the last two days I have experienced no further 'belly aches' and feel that I am somewhat recovering. Keep your fingers crossed!

So as April is being pushed out by a hopefully sunny May I shall just wish you all a more cheerful farewell.

Have a nice Bank Holiday. They seem to be quite frequent nowadays.

Love to you all,
Your 'feeling much better' P.O.G.

* * *

1 May 1994

Dear All,
    May Day. Visions of pretty girls all dressed in white with crowns of primroses dancing around the Maypole. Birds singing and the boys all giggles trying to control an upsurge of awakened hormones. Tip-toe through the tulips. Spring is here.

> The maid who in the first of May
> Goes to the fields at the break of day
> And washes in dew from the hawthorn tree
> Shall ever after handsome be.
>
> Trad. Anon.

    Take heed girls. Arise with the dawn and scamper across the dew-soaked lawn in your bare feet and find the old hawthorn tree. Better than all the Oils of Ulay.
    Sadly times have changed. The girls now dress in skin tight jeans frayed at the hems with holes in the knees. T-shirts emblazoned with, 'Save the Rain Forests', or 'I Love Elvis'. The boys are hardly distinguishable from the girls. Their hair is probably longer and tied back in a ponytail. Mostly they are wanting to go to college to study social-sciences. Parliament is now in the process of legislating new curriculums and proposing 'Condoms for twelve-year-olds'!
    'Playtime children. Don't forget your condoms'!
    A brave new world is emerging and I am being left behind. Press on regardless James! It may never happen.
    We are now in the third week of May and what a month it is turning out to be.
    The Queen has opened the Channel Tunnel. I watched it on the telly. What a wonderful feat of engineering. I must admit that the President of France did not seem over excited about it and his wife looked utterly miserable. The Queen looked radiant and full of *joie de vivre* and was obviously enjoying every moment.
    I also see in my diary that Richard and Nicola turned up on a

154

Sunday evening and forced me to go to the Chequers Inn at Well, where I was made to drink a pint or two of Flowers Bitter. Betty needed no encouraging. She likes Flowers Bitter. I personally think that anyone drinking in public houses on a Sunday is beyond redemption.

They also informed me that Frederick has been lured into proposing Holy Matrimony to a young lady from Weymouth and meets his doom on September the tenth.

Then on Monday the ninth Katie came to show me her engagement ring. Her Dereck has at last dropped on bended knee and proposed. He has been trying to pluck up courage since they finished college ten years ago. Anyway it is a lovely diamond. I hope it doesn't take her another ten years to get him to sign on the dotted line and I do hope that there is not going to be a surfeit of weddings. They are such a drain on the exchequer.

Other news. Our vicar, the Reverend Bill Rogers is leaving us. He is going to take over the parishes of West Lulworth, East Lulworth, Winfrith and Chalden in the county of Dorset. As Lulworth is one of my old hunting grounds I am pleased for him although I think that he has a very difficult task ahead of him. We shall miss him here although he has promised to come back and officiate at my funeral if I last until after he has moved. I have written to my old friend Berty Starr and told him to arrange for the red carpet, the brasses to be polished and the pews dusted before Bill's induction.

The sudden death of John Smith MP has left the Labour Party without a leader. He will be sadly missed. I am so confused with politics. Every day there seems to be a new problem, with politicians confusing the issues for me. The world news goes from bad to worse and there seem to be no solutions to the wars and squabbles that beset it. Poor old World.

Even the weather gets all upset and no two days are the same. Today for instance, being the seventeenth, it has reverted to January. Tomorrow there will most likely be a heat wave. I think that this confusion has become more noticeable with the increase in female weather forecasters. It's the same really with the News.

Now they are talking about privatising the Royal Mail. It seems to me that they are trying to destroy all that is British. I expect we shall be persuaded to buy Eurostamps. It is all in the name of progress. I expect the Americans, Arabs or Japanese will bid for shares and be the controlling bodies. I shall stop writing the 'Letters of P.O.G.'

You may be pleased to know that I have at last received Orders from the NHS. I am to attend Sick Parade at the local hospital on the eighth of June and be X-rayed. They have sent me full instructions and a small bottle of pills to be taken on specific days prior to the appointment. I am also told that I shall be able to drive home after they have finished. They do not specify where the transport is coming from.

Then on the thirteenth I have to parade again and place my body at the disposal of the 'Bellyologist', a Mr Richards. I am told to arrive with a full bladder and deposit the contents into a bottle. The last time I did that I couldn't stop and filled three bottles all marked with different names. You may well laugh but I do not think that it is funny when one's working parts fail to function. Mine, at the time of writing, are what I might term 'spasmodic'. They work in fits and farts.

There is activity next door. My Asian neighbours, Abdullah and Fatima, are displaying signs of a move back to their native land. The garden is being tidied up and MFO (Military Forwarding Organisation) boxes are on the patio ready for the goods and chattels. I wonder whom I shall get next. Eskimos? Red Indians? Zulus? Maybe refugees from Bosnia. Who ever it is I hope that they do not celebrate Ramadan. I shall never get used to the odours of Eastern cooking wafting in during the small hours of the night.

Now I think that I have written enough. The South Africans are now free. Apartheid is no more.

Anything interesting that happens during the week remaining will have to wait until June.

Don't forget to send postcards from those exotic holiday haunts that you will all be going to. I have already had Istanbul (Taffy), and Florida (Rosemary my favourite barlady).

Think of me in the hands of the Bellyologist and keep your

fingers crossed.

Your month older P.O.G.

P.S.

Best wishes from Sam. He has discovered a new hunting gound for large fat mice.

* * *

1 June 1994

Dear Eurocrats,

The last week in May was disastrous. It rained and rained and was unpleasantly cold. Poor Katie having her five days off, camping near Chichester with two or three dogs, lover-boy Dereck and a sailing boat must have felt utterly miserable. I suppose if at the end, she and Dereck were still on talking terms, the exercise proved that even marriage might work.

Calamity also struck Betty. She decided to go to church but arrived without her glasses so she turned round and began to drive back to pick them up. The Flying Daffodil objected and had an argument with another vehicle at the bottom of Church Hill and was severely wounded. Fortunately Betty was unharmed apart from an overdose of shock which left her finding it difficult to speak. The Flying Daffodil has been written-off by the insurance assessor and Betty is now keeping her fingers crossed in the hope that she will be able to get mobile without too much of a delay. She sorely misses her wheels.

Flaming June arrived in splendour. The first day came with glorious sunshine. So hot that I even perspired sitting doing nothing. But not for long. The weatherlady returned to the screen and we are back with a howling gale and heavy showers. As usual rain stopped play on the first day of the Test Match when England seemed to be doing well.

The news is devoted to the forthcoming elections for the European Parliament interspersed with reports of the wars in Bosnia, Africa and all points east and west. Horrific helicopter

157

crash and child abuse together with the usual sexual scandals of the odd MP and pop star.

'D' Day was commemorated over the weekend of the sixth by the BBC in spectacular vision. For my generation it was certainly a trip back into the world of nostalgia but I was left to wonder what our present ethnic population and the new breed of young Britons thought about it all. I wonder if our beloved country was placed in the same danger whether they would band together as we and our parents did. I hope that they will never be faced with such danger.

Now, three days later, we have cast our votes in the new European Parliament Elections. Our politicians have sold us to Europe. Shall we now be governed from Brussels? Shall we see the blue flag with its gold stars replace our Union Jack? Already the European Parliament have condemned our own Parliament for unfair treatment of refuse collectors and other public employees. It seems that Westminster will need to seek permission before any legislation is passed.

Time will tell. My own personal view of Euro-MPs is not encouraging. They seem to spend most of their time shaking hands before the cameras and advertising their dentures. It gives me the impression of a splendid 'Jobs for the Boys and Girls Club'. A lovely cushy number in Brussels.

I doubt very much that my own little cross on the ballot paper will have any effect. For what it's worth we now have a 'Natural Law Party'. I get more bewildered each day.

Enough of that James, Richard, John and Michael now have their hands on the wheel.

Anyway England did win the Test Match and Gooch made a double century.

June at last has found the right weather and we are in the throes of summer as it should be. It seems that we may even have splendid weather for Ascot week.

On a personal note. Angela came on the evening of the seventh to ensure that I got up on the eighth in time to keep my appointment with the X-ray department at the hospital. In true military fashion we paraded five minutes early but in true NHS fashion we sat for the normal long wait before anyone turned up.

158

When they did it was in the person of a very attractive young lady who took me in hand. She was efficient as well as beautiful and soon had me reclining beneath her X-ray in my birthday suit. She was so impressed by my internal organs that she could not stop taking pictures of them. She informed me that my back was twisted and that one kidney was in the wrong place. Amazing. It has taken eighty years for me to discover that I am not as other humans.

At one stage a lady doctor came and pumped some colourless fluid into my arteries after telling me it improved the picture quality. My X-ray beauty then decided that she had taken enough pictures, or else she had run out of film and put the kettle on so that I might have a much needed cup of tea.

The Lady Doctor took me in hand and I was conducted into another room and forced into another position flat on my back. My stomach area was painted with some form of unction and the Doctor donned a pair of headphones and began taking a series of sound readings from my internal organs. The same test apparently that is given to pregnant women. I was relieved to know that I was not in that condition.

And that was the end of the ordeal. Angela drove me in a semi-conscious state to the Anchor Inn where I was revived with a pint of Hardy Country Ale.

The follow up came on Monday the thirteenth. John arrived to take me for my appointment with the Surgeon Consultant. I had to arrive with a full bladder and empty it into a bottle. It was very difficult because the bottle was merely a small phial. Then Mr Richards – that was his name – began an investigation of my nether regions after a lengthy interrogation and a study of the X-ray pictures taken as described above.

He then told me that he would have to arrange for me to present myself to him at Basingstoke Hospital so that he could open me up and have a look inside. He did not say why. I got the impression that it was either mere curiosity or that something was where it shouldn't be. He then handed me back to the nurse who tried to get a blood sample from my left arm without any success. No blood. She did manage after a great effort to suck some from my right arm. I was quite amazed because when I cut myself shaving it flows quite freely. Perhaps I have no blood from the neck down.

Now it is just a question of 'wait' until I see my own doctor next week. Maybe she will know more of what it is all about.

Now I must stop. Hunger calls me to the kitchen and I wish to see the start of Royal Ascot.

I will keep you informed regarding my medical progress.

The garden is looking very gay and colourful. Don't forget your wornout,

P.O.G.

* * *

9 September 1994

Dear All,

The last two weeks of June are on the threshold. On the thirteenth I saw the Bellyologist, a very brutal man who subjected me to a new dimension of physical torture. Fortunately I had John to rescue me and revive me after the ordeal by driving me to the Anchor Inn. What would I do without Hardy Country Ale.

Then three days later I received a summons to report to Basingstoke Hospital on Wednesday the twenty-second. I felt a certain degree of fright and rang Doctor Moore who calmly told me that I ought to keep the appointment. My belly needs looking at. I only hope that my Bellyologist is more gentle with his operating than his diagnosing. And there you have it. Angela is coming to deliver me into his hands. The last time that she delivered me into a surgeon's clutches there was a frightful snowstorm and sub-zero weather. I caught the foulest of colds and arrived at the Military Hospital in Woolwich at death's door. I hope she is more successful this time.

Fortunately the weather forecast seems more favourable, although with Wimbledon tennis just starting it will probably revert to howling gales and rain. At least Ascot week was held on glorious sunshine. The ladies all donned great wide brimmed millinery concoctions, wore short skirts and exposed

160

their bony knees. Many looked like human mushrooms. So very few women have beautiful legs. Anyway the horses were pictures of health.

Again, after winning the First Test Match our English team has reverted to their usual form. They just managed to avoid a follow-on in the Second Test at Lords and are now praying for rain to help them make a draw. Perhaps they will have a better second innings.

It is now the twenty-first. The summer solstice. The longest day. England did just manage to hang on and make a draw and now that Wimbledon fortnight has started the weather has reverted to its anti-tennis state. Rain has already stopped play during the opening set of the first ladies' match.

British Rail are starting a series of one-day strikes just to add to the mayhem on the roads, and tomorrow I shall be reclining in a hospital bed. At least I shall be letting someone else do all the worrying. Now I have nothing further to say. With luck I shall finish this and give you details of my ordeal in Basingstoke. Keep your fingers crossed and if you pray to our maker ask Him to keep an eye on P.O.G.

June, July, August and the first two weeks of September have melted into the past. The best summer that we have experienced for years and I was incarcerated in hospital and convalescent homes, and from the twenty-second day of June the sun shone over this green and pleasant land.

And so, the year 1994 will henceforth be known as the year of the wasted summer.

I now have only hazy remembrances of those sun-filled months. I remember, for instance, the twenty-second of June when Angela delivered me to Basingstoke Hospital. The surprise we both felt at the VIP treatment on arrival with a private room and bathroom 'en suite'. I remember Sister Alison Jupp who took me in charge so efficiently. The strange lady who floated silently in carrying a little tray of phials demanding samples of my blood. She became such a frequent visitor that I could only think of her as the Basingstoke Vampire. A succession of nurses descended on me to inject me with something they said would prevent my blood from coagulating. This seemed to take place at half-hourly intervals. When Sister Alison Jupp came and began to cover my manly chest with electrodes Angela decided to leave me to my fate.

And the sun shone from that day forth in all its glory and I began to know what caged animals in the zoo felt like. I watched Wimbledon on the television between injections and blood sucking.

Mr Richards, the Surgeon, came happily in to say that he would be looking inside me the very next day. He seemed excited at the prospect. I was then lured into the dungeons for a chest X-ray which I gathered was to discover my fitness for anaesthetics. Back in my room a giant visited me. The Anaesthetist. He must have been six-and-a-half feet tall, four feet wide and bearded like some ancient Briton – except that he was French. He promptly told me that they had decided that I was to have a local anaesthetic because of the unhealthy state of my chest, but not to worry, I wouldn't feel a thing.

I was starved from then on until I was made ready for the theatre. I wonder why they call it a theatre. I saw nothing of the show and heard no applause. I awoke back in my room to find myself plumbed in to something I could not see and a vast array of plastic piping sprouting from my most private regions. From then on it seemed to be nothing but discomfort and a continual flushing of my internal waterworks. I drank a gallon of water and watched Wimbledon although I could not tell you now who won what.

Mr Richards came to see me the next day and when I asked what he had found inside me he promptly said, 'Rubbish', which I did not think was encouraging.

My next recollection was of a very black nurse who said she came from the Philippines. Whether or not she was imported just for my benefit I know not, but I could not understand what she was saying, having at that moment removed my hearing aids. She wrote on a large board and I read 'We shall be removing your plumbing at midnight.'

The clock struck twelve and there she was with another nurse and a sadistic look on her face. I could not see what they were

162

doing but they said it would not hurt. I think she stood on my chest, grasped the internal plumbing and heaved. I swear my personal pride and joy was stretched to the limit. One more pull and it would have come off altogether. My instructions then were to pass my water into the bottle provided whenever I felt so inclined. From vague recollections I seem to remember days and nights spent using bottles which were promptly removed and the contents measured.

There was a semi-crisis on the first morning that I could shower and dress. I had a tap thing taped to my wrist giving access to an artery. I pulled on a pair of pants and slipped a vest over my head and Bingo! The tap thing flew off and blood flew everywhere; all over my nice clean vest and pants, the walls, the floor. In fact the Basingstoke Vampire would have had a veritable feast, but unfortunately she was not around. I pulled the 'panic button' and fled to the bathroom where I did my best to stop the blood with my face-flannel. Sister Alison quickly took charge and within minutes I was plugged up and the excess blood was washed from the walls, carpets and me. Panic over.

Mr Richards' next visit provided more information regarding my inside: a malignant growth in my bladder which he could only partly remove. He wished me to see one of his colleagues who specialised in radio therapy – a Doctor Ryall. And so I was introduced to another advance in medical cures. Doctor Ryall was a superb salesman. It could do me no harm. It could only do good. I could be cosseted in the luxurious convalescent home at Netley Castle. I would be transported with no worries and although he could not guarantee removing the evil growth, it could be contained. He sold the treatment to me and I agreed to place myself in his hands.

At this stage I was not in any condition to care for myself so it was decided that I would go to Angela's until they sent for me to go to Netley. And the day came for my discharge from Basingstoke. I had of course been visited by all my friends and relations although the days and times elude me. I do remember John, who came well after visiting hours were over and brought me a magnificent bunch of roses from his new garden.

163

Pauline was to rescue me from the hospital and take me home to Bentley where Angela would pick me up and cart me off to Tollard Royal. I persuaded Pauline to first take me to the bank and then to the Anchor for a medicinal pint of Hardy Country Ale.

I remember the drive with Angela only too well. I foolishly did not use the toilet before we started the journey and from Salisbury onwards I sat with my legs crossed breaking my neck in an effort not to soil my pants. We just made it.

Next came Netley. They were to collect me on my birthday and take me to Southampton Hospital for my first ordeal at the radiotherapy department and then on to the castle. John's remark as soon as he knew that I would be going to Netley was:

'I always knew that you would end up in a padded cell, Dad!'

Netley had been the military psychiatric hospital and was commonly known as the 'Nut House'. However, Netley Castle turned out to be a splendid place in which to relax and be cared for. I was transported for my treatment sessions into the hospital in Southampton. I again had visitors who I feel came more out of curiosity to see the castle than me.

Treatment ended. Angela and her neighbour Gill arrived to cart me back to Tollard. Then the rot set in.

I was at this stage informed that certain unpleasant side effects would occur. Bowel upsets which developed into a near dysentery. I could not eat fruit or green vegetables. In fact it seemed that there was little that I was allowed to eat. My sense of taste would probably not return to normal for some months. There were other discomforts which are best forgotten.

At least while I was with Angela I made some new friends. Her neighbours Dereck and Gill Nelson were so kind. It is always nice to meet wonderful people and the Nelsons were and are certainly that. I felt honoured and grateful at the same time. Gill's lovely mother visiting was also utterly charming.

And now I am back home in Bentley where Betty has been holding the fort. She is still in charge and checks daily to see that I am still living. Sam was pleased to see me back although

164

complained that I reeked of dogs and horses. And so now, with my inside slowly becoming normal I am gradually improving, and perhaps by Christmas I shall recognise the taste of Lambs Navy Rum and Hardy Country Ale.

So now I must just remain,

Your still somewhat costive P.O.G.

P.S.

Doctor Ryall must be sure that I shall survive the year because he sent me an appointment card for the twenty-seventh of January 1995 . . . .

So, as I stated earlier, the summer of 1994 passed me by.

British Rail are still disrupting travel with two-day strikes. England's cricketers put up a good show and the world has changed little. Except that more troubles have erupted in new places.

The toilet awaits me!

* * *

4 October 1994

Dear All,

The last nine months of 1994 have not been very pleasant to say the least, and now here I am back at No. 17 Eggars Field endeavouring to pick up the reins and put my aged bones back into some form of normality. I make the effort to force my legs into gear, so far only first, and stagger down to the village shop every day. Every person that I meet greets me with a smile and informs me that they are pleased to see me back looking a picture of health. This surprises me. I arrive back home and look in the mirror. I see a haggard broken down old hack and conclude that the villagers of Bentley need to visit the Optician. Still it is good to be back in my own home and puff my way up my own staircase. Betty has polished, dusted and cleaned, nurtured Sam, cared for the garden, got a new car to replace the old Flying Daffodil (which got involved in an argument with other vehicles and was written off) and in general has kept the 'home fires burning'.

I did get home in time to pick my own runner beans and enjoy the odd feast of blackberries.

My neighbours, Abdullah and Fatima, have, I think, gone back to Borneo or wherever they came from. They went on the last day of September. I shall miss the aroma of Eastern nosh wafting in at odd hours of the day and night especially during Ramadan. I now wonder who I shall get next. So far I've had English, American and Irish. In this now ethnic society I shall not be surprised whatever nationality they are.

Since arriving home I have had visits from many old friends all wanting to take me out for lunch. Tony and Heather Rudin came with exciting tales of global adventures. Angela, Richard and Susan on different days, and a pleasant surprise when Frederick and his Jacky popped in after their wedding on their way to Gatwick to fly off to Florida on their honeymoon. They brought me some wedding cake and both looked wonderfully happy. The fourth in the line of 'Maudie Dowdeswells', I was pleased to note was a most attractive successor. My own Maudie would have approved.

And so I am working hard to get fit again. A slow process. I have reservations about the healing qualities of radio therapy and I now know what a poor unfortunate chicken feels like when it is cooked in a microwave oven. Some of the after-effects of the treatment are noticeably better although my taste-buds are still faulty. I drop off to sleep at frequent intervals, my loo visits are still more frequent than I would like but as the works are functioning I suppose I must be grateful.

Television programmes have got worse. We seem to be in the clutches of American rubbish, Australian soaps and a glut of feminism, *Birds of a Feather* etc. Even the sports commentators are female now. *Songs of Praise* is now generally broadcast from foreign parts; Harvest Festival from the vineyards of France. Have you ever sung *We Plough the Fields* in French with English sub-titles? Football dominates the sporting world and so we are reduced to videos. I think the BBC has a vested interest in their sales.

Now I must stop. I am still expecting the million from Ernie.

166

There is no harm in expecting.

Be good to one another and I am always here waiting to be taken out to lunch.

The leaves are fluttering down and the garden is being tucked up for the winter – by Betty I might add.

As ever, (Sorry, not quite as ever),
P.O.G.

* * *

25 October 1994

Dear All,

Still October. I know that I grumbled about being locked up in hospital for the summer but I must now say that the Weatherman has relented and I am now in one of the most perfect autumns that I have experienced for many years. Gorgeous sunny days with just that encouraging nip in the air and all the trees changing into their autumn colours. I am told that we have had early-morning frosts but I regret to say that slothful habits kept me beneath my duvet. Betty has tidied the garden, planted bulbs, wallflowers and winter pansies so that it is now tucked up for the winter yet to come. She has also seen to Theresa Mona, removed the geraniums and replanted with winter pansies. So we are well on the way to finish our preparations to see us through the winter.

I seem to be improving healthwise, almost daily. My main problem now is puffing. I need new bellows but I'm afraid I shall have to put up with what I have and just keep puffing.

Now. What have I got to write about? I shall not in future bore you with my medical problems.

One problem that has been worrying me for some time has been bacon. As you know bacon today is sold in flaccid, vacuum-packed plastic. I have now discovered, to my great delight, that the real thing is now available via mail order. I read in a magazine entitled *Oldie* that a gentleman named Chris Battle, who runs the Jack Scaife butcher's shop in Keighley, West Yorkshire, has been home curing bacon for his family and

167

friends and a few selected customers for the past twenty years. I quote Chris Battle:

> Modern bacon is factory produced and involves a saline solution being injected into the pork carcass. The solution is 90 per cent water. When this sort of bacon is cooked it shrinks and leaves a white scum in the pan.

Mr Battle prepares bacon in the traditional way. It takes longer, but he does not use any chemicals or inject it with water. His bacon does not shrink when it is cooked and you are not paying for water and chemicals. He likes to discuss with customers exactly how they like their bacon – how thick the rashers are, how much lean, how much fat and so forth. He will send out orders as small as half-a-pound, but points out that larger orders save postage, because traditionally cured bacon will keep in an ordinary fridge for up to six months.

So there you have it. For bespoke bacon, call Mr Battle on 0535 605808. If you think I am joking come over for breakfast one morning. No more white scum in the pan.

Now. What other gems have I learned of late? Oh Yes. An *Alternative Biography*.

THATCHER, (MARGARET) HILDA, MBE. Born Margaret Hilda Roberts in Grantham, Lincs in 1925. She took a degree in science before reading for the Bar with a view to entering politics. She was discouraged by the failure of her first attempt to win a seat in Parliament and with her husband Denis Thatcher entered the world of ballroom dancing, a pursuit on which she was to leave her inimitable stamp. They became Home Counties champions for the first time in 1954 and UK champions in 1959, when they also claimed the BBC *Come Dancing* 'Twosome of the Tournament' title. A world title eluded them although Margaret herself when partnered briefly by the American Al Haig became

Latin-American champion in 1982.

From 1979 she directed the Hilda Thatcher Formation Dancers, who remained unbeatable until 1990.

Would you believe it? I must admit it surprised me.

A surprise visit from Georgia did a lot to lift me out of the 'slough of despair'. She arrived at teatime and was lucky because I had some scones left over from the previous day plus cream and strawberry jam. I was pleased also to meet her friend, Annie, who was doing the driving. I do like surprise visits.

Any day now I am expecting a new neighbour. I understand that it is to be a lady. I hope that she will be English and beautiful. Exciting isn't it?

I have little news from the rest of the family apart from my dear sister Hilda Margaret who is going through a 'falling over' epidemic. Twice in a few days she has come to grief. Black-eyes, bruised arms and lots of bumps. She tells me that the black-eyes are the least of her wounds and at least get her sympathy from all her friends. Why is it that elderly ladies are always in such a hurry?

Now it is time for me to practise some of my culinary skills. A shepherd's pie sounds tempting.

Father Christmas has arrived in Surrey and Hampshire. I think he must be getting confused with the seasons. Don't forget to put your clocks back.

Spring forward. Fall back.

Love one another and sweep up all those dead leaves.

Your still here P.O.G.

* * *

23 November 1994

No warmth, no cheerfulness, no healthful ease.
No comfortable feel in any member –
No shade, no shine, no butterflies, no bees,

169

No fruits, no flowers, no leaves, no birds,
November!

Anon

Dear All,

It has been a very, very strange month. I have vague recollections of happenings in the early days. I remember that the Lady Farrier came and attended to my pedal extremities. My barber came and gave me a short back and sides and discussed the problems besetting the village and the world in general. He is the complete pessimist.

It was half term and I went out for a lunch with Pauline, Holly and Chloe. It was a fine, sunny day although quite chilly. There were also two young ladies aged around ten years who knocked on my door and surprised me with, 'James. Is there any housework that you would like us to do for you?'

As Betty had already dusted and polished I had to refuse their kind offer and reward them with Funsize Mars Bars.

I vaguely remember seeing on the News that Mr Kinnock was taking up the post of Commissioner to the European Parliament in Brussels with the meagre salary of around £100,000 per annum. He will no doubt be a lord before the year is out. My mind flickered to all the other defunct politicians who had become lords. I haven't heard much about Peace Negotiator Lord Owen lately. His war still seems to be thriving.

Jobs for the boys.

May I now quote a rhyme from my youth:

Please to remember
The Fifth of November,
Gunpowder, treason and plot;
I know no reason
Why gunpowder treason
Should ever be forgot.

There is every reason. In Bentley the fireworks started on the third and continued nightly until the seventh. Sam was very upset. He spent every evening hiding under the bed.

170

It was about this time that I was attacked by the GERM. It sneaked upon me from a little sniffing and hacking cough and developed into a near fatal flu. Clever James thought that he could cure it without resorting to the Doctor. Foolish James. I really did nearly surrender one night when I was fighting for breath.

Angela's arrival took the reins out of my hands and Doctor Way was summoned. She immediately put me on a diet of antibiotics and I entered a stage of pill induced euphoria. Which is why this letter is full of hazy recollections. I slowly returned to the land of the living and at this moment of time I am fairly normal – at least as normal as can be expected. I shall have to make an appointment to see the Doctor and thank her for saving my life.

The great National Lottery was launched and the whole country has gone raving mad. Money is now sharing first place with sex. I remember in my youth when history lessons covered the fall of the Roman Empire, how the Roman Emperor and his minions appeased the starving populace by putting on fabulous shows with gladiators carving one another up and Christians being thrown to the lions. The big boys cantered round Rome in their chariots tossing shekels and the odd gold coin for the poor and needy to grovel for.

Our politicians have improved on that with football matches and now lotteries. Every day thousands of pounds and luxurious motor cars together with holidays of a lifetime are offered as prizes in television game shows. I'm sure that it is only done to keep the populace quiet and their minds off the mess that the world is in. I shall probably win the 'Jackpot' next week.

Religion too is taking on a new dimension and new sit-coms are starting with the antics of women vicars. *Songs of Praise* last week was quite enlightening. It came from a packed Victoria Palace Theatre, London, with stage stars leading the singing of modern hymns: *Come on and Celebrate* and *How Great Thou Art*. I was most impressed by the latter. The congregation really let rip with *How Great Thou Art.*' Those four words were the only words in the hymn and were screamed to a modern beat in continuous repetition accenuated by vigorous hand-clapping. I could almost see Old Lordy sitting up aloft sticking His chest out as all this acclaim reached His ears.

'They really do love me,' I could hear Him say. This week it was quite thrilling with a great host of children singing their praises as an introduction to the 'Children in Need' appeal being launched by the BBC.

It is all very confusing for a doddery old man.

My new neighbour has taken up residence. I have not been neighbourly and invited her in for coffee because I was afraid of spreading the GERM. I think that she has a dog and a cat but I don't know for sure. I shall soon have to start being nosy and ooze out my charm. I know her name is Deborah but nothing else.

You will be pleased to know that I have now installed a modern communications system. British Telecom have fitted me out with a new phone placed so that I can reach it from my chair. It has a built-in memory so that I don't even have to dial the important numbers. I just press a button and it automatically dials Angela or Richard and anyone else that had been entered into its brain. It also has an adjustable bell that I can hear. I also have a deaf-aid bell in the hall. I shall probably get the Fire Brigade when that rings. And you won't believe this, I have a phone by my bedside so that I can now scream for help if and when I need it in the night. Mind you, I don't know yet if any of this works because no one rings me up now.

I must end on a sad note. As you all know Michael's Mary passed away after a long terminal illness. One can say that she is now free from pain but it is still sad for her loved ones. She was a very brave woman and Michael will miss her. He will be in all our prayers and thoughts.

Now I must away and be about my business. That will mean switching on the telly and wafting off into my afternoon nap. I suffer from spasmodic insomnia if you can work that out.

Be good. Christmas will soon be with us and the geese are quite fat.

Nearly as ever, but not quite,

Your affectionate P.O.G.

14 December 1994

What should we speak of
When you are as old as me? When shall we hear
The rain and wind beat dark December, how,
In this my pinching cave, shall we discourse
The freezing hours away.

Shakespeare.

Dear All,

Where did November go? December began pleasantly mild and my 'Pinching cave' enhanced by a visit from Eirene and Leslie who I persuaded to take me to lunch at the Anchor Inn. As we had not met for some two years or so there was a great deal of family news to exchange. I shall be some while recovering.

The Post delivered a very interesting 'Down-Under' Christmas card from my niece Thelma, together with some lovely photos and a most enlightening letter. Thelma tells me that they are beset with politicians of much the same calibre as ours. Her descriptions were not flattering. At least the photos of her children and herself proved that altogether we are a very handsome family.

The politicians are apparently planning to privatise all the public services and Thelma does not approve. At least she won't also be burdened with value-added tax on fuels and everything else that we are suffering.

While I am on the subject of politics you may be interested in a small item that I read somewhere concerning the EC. It may give you food for thought about what being in the European Union means.

The Lord's Prayer has 58 words.
The Ten Commandments have 207 words.

The American Declaration of Independence has 310 words.
But the EC directive on the exporting of duck eggs has 28,911 words!

Mr Major and his Chancellor were defeated in the House over the increase of VAT on fuel. So he has produced a Mini Budget and bunged it all on cigarettes and booze. Good idea. One doesn't have to smoke and the amount of the other that I drink will hardly affect. Unfortunately he has put a little more on petrol. The AA spokesman aptly accused the Chancellor of using the motorist as a 'wallet on wheels'. The country's Economy seems to get worse. I believe that they have only just paid for the cannon balls used at the Battle of Waterloo. As I now have no car the only protest I have heard has been from Betty. It would do Mr Major good to hear Betty when she gets on her 'soap box'. Her views on the affairs in Brussels must scorch his ears.

And did you know that Father Christmas in Australia wears sandals instead of snow boots? I've got a card from 'Down-Under' to prove it. And what has that got to do with it?

There is no limit to my knowledge! I learn something new every day.

I nearly started on a bleat about the EC but Christmas is all 'Peace on Earth and Good Will' so I will leave the affairs in Brussels until 1995 – if I'm still around, and contain my feelings of frustration until then. Just remember:

'Don't let Europe Rule Britannia'.

The National Lottery has got off to a rip roaring start with eighteen million pounds going to the jackpot winner this week. My own chances are improving. In the first week I never had a single number right. Last week I picked one. At that rate of progress I should get the six correct by the second week in 1995.

The Queen has struck oil in Windsor Great Park. Lucky Queen. She won't mind being made redundant now.

Only ten shopping days left before Christmas. My own gifts are parcelled up and ready for Father Christmas to collect and deliver. I have posted all my greetings cards and as usual received two today from friends that I had forgotten. It always happens.

So now all that remains is for me to finish by wishing you all a very Happy Christmas and a Splendid and Prosperous New Year.

I leave you with a little thought from Sir Walter Scott in 1788.

England was merry England when,
Old Christmas brought his sports again,
T'was Christmas broach'd the mightiest ale,
T'was Christmas told the merriest tale:
A Christmas gambol oft would cheer
The poor man's heart through half the year.

So, all of you, prepare to have a good old gambol and broach the mightiest ale – now £16 per gallon!

God Bless you one and all,
                    Your hopefully festive P.O.G.

*   *   *

THE LETTERS OF P.O.G.
1995

3 January 1995

The soul's dark cottage, batter'd and decay'd,
Lets in new light through chinks that time has made;
Stronger by weakness, wiser men become,
As they draw near to their eternal home.
Leaving the old, both worlds at once they view,
That stand upon the threshold of the new.
                    Edmund Waller. 1606-1687.

Dear All,

That's me. Old P.O.G. Standing on the threshold of the New Year with a new light shining through the chinks that time has made. The struggle for survival continues and I only hope that 1995 is kinder than 1994. Anyway the sun is shining this morning and I am beginning to feel alive once more.

Christmas is now a Christmas past and I spent it happily with Angela and David. I seemed to do little but unwrap gift after gift. To thank each of you individually would keep me occupied until the cows come home which will be a long time. So 'Thank you, one and all'. One from Holly and Chloe must have a mention. A green frog soap which if I wash until the soap vanishes, will produce me a handsome prince! I wonder if I can change it for a princess?

We are starting 1995 without wheels. Betty did some ice skating with a rather large Rover and her little Metro suffered a broken nose. We hope that the insurance people will not be too long before she is mobile again.

Sam is pleased that it is all over. Too many visitors interfere with his sleep. My new neighbours also have a cat and a dog and Sam showed his disapproval in no uncertain manner when the little cat decided to pay a courtesy call. Aiden and Debra came in for mince pies and rum punch. They are very nice people. Three children. Girls. Emma, Rachel and another Emma who answers to 'Small'.

There will be an intermission now as my door bell is ringing.

179

No doubt someone hoping for coffee.

Excuse me for a while.

I'm back. It was. Old friends of Betty. I had to ask them in to wait until she returned from her labours. My sherry decanter is empty. Anyway they were nice people and I enjoyed entertaining them.

I have also forgotten what I was going to write about. I know that I discarded any intention of making New Year resolutions which my dictionary tells me are : 'Good intentions that one formulates mentally for virtuous conduct.' As my conduct is always virtuous I am obviously excused.

My horoscope tells me that Jupiter and Pluto are operating very much in my favour and a power greater than myself is bringing to fruition seeds that were planted many moons ago. I shall probably turn into a cabbage although I would prefer something more attractive. A Busy Lizzie perhaps.

Samson continues to prove what a very educated and intelligent cat he is. As you may know Betty takes *The Sun* newspaper which is something I cannot understand. She came in the other morning and dropped it on the doormat. She decided to leave it there and retrieve it as she went out. Samson happened to see it. He immediately jumped on it and tore it to shreds. I keep telling Betty that she should take *The Telegraph* Sam would probably do the crossword for her.

What a strange month January is. It is a 'nothing' month. Everything seems dormant. And the weather has turned nasty. Windy, cold and wet. And news from the rest of the world is much the same. Utterly depressing. In this fair isle of ours the prisons are overflowing and escaping murderers are making headlines. The Animal Rights People are making violent demonstrations at the ports over the exporting of livestock. In a way I sympathise with them but must condemn the violence they are using. It does not help the poor sheep and cattle and only makes more work for our already stretched police force. It seems to me that demonstrating is a new sport and no aspect of our existence is safe. There is always someone with an objection to something or other. I shall object to objectors. Join my society for the 'Suppression of Mirth and the Promotion of Misery'

Anyone found smiling will be sent to Coventry. Or Birmingham if they prefer it.

I'm twaddling again. Forgive me. This is really supposed to be a thank you letter so I will leave it with once again wishing you all a wonderful 1995.

Perhaps by the end of the month something really interesting will happen for me to write about. Who knows? Perhaps I shall win the Lottery.

As I close I see that the sun is shining.

Hooray! I shall wend my way to ye olde village store and get some dry ginger ale for my rum.

Your still on the threshold P.O.G.

* * *

24 January 1995

I am a very foolish, fond old man,
Fourscore and upward, not an hour more or less;
And, to deal plainly,
I fear I am not in my perfect mind.

William Shakespeare. King Lear.

Dear All,

It is very true. Age is deceptive. Take Susan. She has been forty-seven years old since 1993 whereas my dear sister Hilda Margaret will be eighty-eight years old on the twenty-first of March but eighty-nine on the twenty-second. I have an idea that I may be wrong there. She may be eighty-nine years old on the twenty-first which will make her ninety on the twenty-second.

I leave you to work all that out.

Another thing that I find confusing is why biscuit tins are always made rectangular. Why can they not be square? Whenever I return the lid to a tin I always have to turn it to make it fit.

You now see the reason for my quoting the great Bard. I have an imperfect mind.

181

Richard and Nicola, I am given to understand, are the first members of the family to venture under the English Channel and travel to Paris on *Le Shuttle*. They apparently went over for an evening meal and tell me that the journey was an exciting experience. The fact that they returned with a near fatal dose of food poisoning just proves that the French cannot be trusted. Richard also told me that he noticed a number of jackbooted men all speaking German, behaving somewhat strangely. It was probably a party of senior German officers in the throes of a TEWT with the feasible object of a future invasion of Britain.

Richard wonders if they can sleep safely in their beds. Not if he intends to continue eating in Paris! For those non-military TEWT stands for: 'Tactical Exercise Without Troops'. For anyone interested I can forward the detailed plans for the Subjection of England by the Fourth Reich. Just send an SAE and I will give it consideration. Do not apply unless you have signed the Official Secrecy Act.

A further interesting piece of news came from Hermione in the form of a press-cutting from the *Guernsey Evening News* relating to the Island of Alderney. The powers that be in that idyllic island have now discovered that they are infested with rats. It has already taken them twenty years or more to discover this unpleasant fact. I, as a matter of interest, brought it to their notice before Maudie and I left the Island around 1975. The place was alive with rats then so I can well imagine that they now have a major problem on their hands. I shall write and recommend that they send an SOS to the Burgomaster of the town of Hamelin where the same problem arose many years ago. I think that they still keep a Pied Piper on the staff.

You will be pleased to know that Betty has her little car back from the Vehicle Hospital. It is resplendent in a new bonnet, a special treble strength bumper and a new headlight. I suggested that she had a cow catcher type of deterrent fitted but she thought that it might be safer if I walked in front with a red flag. Really even to venture forth these days takes all one's courage. Anyway it is nice to know that she is mobile again.

The weather has turned really foul with high winds and torrential rain. Pauline came over to take me out for lunch on the nineteenth and we made it to the Anchor Inn. The trouble started on the return journey and we eventually spluttered to a standstill on the crossroads in Bentley. The rain had won. We had to abandon ship and splash our way home via the village store where I had to stop and get my breath back. Pauline was eventually rescued from No. 17 by Andy. I hope the experience does not put her off visiting me in the future. We naturally experienced the usual power failure that invariably happens when we get anything more than a high wind. I suppose really we must consider ourselves fortunate. We could be Japanese. The most horrific earthquake for many years has devastated great areas in the south of the Islands causing many thousands of deaths and homeless survivors. There always seems to be someone much worse-off than ourselves.

The last week of January. Angela is coming up on the twenty-seventh to escort me to my appointment with the Bellyologist for what I trust will be a final check-up. My inside works seem to be functioning better than before. Well, except my bellows that still wheeze something 'orrid. I will inform you of the findings of Doctor Ryalls in my February letter. If I get that far.

I need the attention of a barber. That is another luxury that we poor males have been deprived of. No barbers. Only unisex salons. Surprisingly I found what was advertised as a genuine gents barber in Alton and drifted in. There actually was a male barber working. But, wait for it, the rest of the staff comprised two young ladies. One was just off for lunch and the other was doing wonders on the head of a modern young man. She was styling his hair into a forest of upright spikes. Naturally she was going to see to me. I begged her not to consider any artistic design on my hair which made her laugh. 'Which hair?' she queried sarcastically Anyway she did a swift short back and sides with electric clippers, charged me OAP half price and I was away within five minutes. Gone are the days when we males could luxuriate in the Barber's chair, have a hair-cut and a shave with hot towels and listen to the Barber's pearls of wisdom. The ladies are winning hands down.

My electric clothes drier also went kaput after twenty years or so of service and I have been obliged to have a new one installed. As with all modern appliances it came complete with a most confusing set of instructions. I should say ambiguous. Anyway this morning I have set the thing in motion and am now going to stop this twaddle and see what has happened to my weekly wash. If there are any mistakes in the above it is because I find it difficult to work this word processor with my fingers crossed.

Be good now and think sometimes of your 'struggling to survive'.

P.O.G.

*   *   *

10 February 1995

Dear All,

You will all be pleased to hear, I hope, that Dr Ryall examined his handiwork and pronounced me fit from the waist downwards. He is satisfied that apart from the reproductive angle, all my nether parts are in good shape. It seems unlikely that I shall ever be able like Abraham, who together with the aid of his wife Sarah, produced a son named Isaac when they were both around one hundred years old. That sort of exercise would probably put the final touches to P.O.G. though perhaps it might be a pleasant way to go.

Mind you, the area of my being from the waist to the neck, which contains my bellows and the main engine, is a lot below standard and in a dodgy condition. I wheeze, and so far this year I have not got out of first gear. From the neck up there are also problems. The few teeth that remain, more or less five I think, cause me to exist on porridge and bread and butter puddings. The little grey cells, as Monsieur Poirot calls them, are also deteriorating daily as will be obvious to you if you have read this far. I can still find the strength to lift a pint of Hardy Country Ale to my lips if anyone would care to come and take me to the Anchor Inn.

I am reminded as I glance at my calendar that Ramadan (subject to the sighting of the moon) commenced on the first. I

184

shall miss the odours of Eastern nosh that drifted down my chimney at all hours of darkness when Abdullah and Fatima were my neighbours. I think that Debra and Aiden and the three girls must eat out. Macdonalds probably. I have not heard, smelt or seen anything of them since Christmas. Maybe I shall when the spring gets here.

For some unknown reason I allowed myself to delve into the writings of Psychiatrist Sigmund Freud which should let you know that I am not quite all there. He emphasises that sex is the primary motivating force of the human race. He is out of date. Sex is being pushed into second place by the lust for money. I have even been lured into joining the madness of the National Lottery and squandering my £1 each week in the hopes of becoming a millionaire. The television quiz shows with astronomical cash prizes dominate the daily programmes. Quiz calls after every programme invite me to ring 0981 33 55 33 or some such number and test my knowledge:

'In which country is the River Thames?

Is it France – Egypt – or England?'

Calls cost only 48p per minute at off-peak times. If my answer is correct and the first received out of ten million I could win the holiday of a lifetime to Disney Land and in Florida or Down-Under to see Sydney Opera House or even the Bahamas.

Are we all going mad?

Yes we are! If you need further proof just switch on to *Westminster Live* and listen to our elected members of Parliament. A single Eurocurrency is the issue being haggled over. I have only just got used to 'Decimalisation' and still think mainly in terms of the good old days of pounds, shillings and pence.

There are many other issues being haggled over: Northern Ireland; export of live cattle; privatisation of everything they can think of; bigger pay rises for company directors; more pay, longer holidays and smaller classes for teachers; pollution everywhere from our beaches to our inner cities; crime. Join the Neighbourhood Watch and clap hands when you see a burglar.

I could go on. What are you going to do about it? I would be

185

interested in your views. I am lost. As I stated earlier my mind is boggled and feeble.

Poor old England. At least we seem to have a rugby fifteen.

But it is not a new situation. It was much the same in 1895. I quote a gentleman named Alan Patrick Herbert:

Well, fancy giving money to the Government!
    Might as well have put it down the drain.
Fancy giving money to the Government!
    Nobody will see the stuff again.
Well, they've no idea what money's for—
    ten to one they'll start another war.
I've heard a lot of silly things, but, Lor'!
    Fancy giving money to the Government.

The only trouble is that we don't seem to have much choice. We could of course vote for Lord Sutch.

This month of February at least is not quite so much a burden on my exchequer birthday-wise. Just one. Angela celebrated her Heinz Variety day on the sixth. I hear that she had a very happy day.

I am now lost for words. I can think no more.
                    'England Needs You.'
I am thinking of becoming a hermit and taking up my theological studies that I commenced in 1993 and lost heart when I reached the dreadful goings on of Lot. I wonder if Abraham might be an interesting subject.

No more now.

                    Your frustrated, useless P.O.G.

                    * * *
                        .

                                    28 February 1995

There was an old man from Bentley,
Who listened very intently,

186

But the words to his brain
Just failed to remain,
That forgetful old man from Bentley.

Dear All,

Shrove Tuesday. Pancakes and another February down the drain. St Valentine's Day was hardly noticed. Last year the BBC had a sexual orgy. This year only a gentle reminder of 'Romance'.

Anyway, being the forgetful old man that I am, I can remember very little of what has happened during the past weeks. I am trying hard to remember what I am supposed to be doing today.

A week ago I was forced to send an SOS out for Doctor Way. A disgusting, revolting, body-wracking germ infected my main engine and left me spluttering and gasping for breath. Antibiotics she said. Antibiotics I swallowed. Pints of gooey fluid looking like treble cream erupted from my poor, worn-out old body.

Yesterday I felt worse. Another SOS. Doctor Way was out on an emergency and unavailable but Doctor Moore himself arrived with the 7th Cavalry. In a horrid croaking fashion I tried to explain the symptoms of my discomfort to him. He lost no time in running his expert fingers over my wasted carcass. I like Doctor Moore. He apologised for his icy cold hands and proposed a change of antibiotics so I am back where I started last week.

One white pill first thing each day followed by red pills at regular intervals until bedtime. The white pills are to keep me frequently in the loo. The red pills are to fight the evil infection in my chest.

HELP!

Now I can only wait and see if it all works.

Excuse me a moment while I pop to the loo.

Now I've forgotten what I was supposed to be writing about. I haven't anything to write about. Betty is doing my shopping today and still keeping her eye on me.

One thing that I have noticed since I had a telephone installed upstairs as well as down. I can almost see my prospective callers standing and thinking. 'Ah! He is at the bottom of the stairs. I'll count seven and then ring.'

And there I am like the Grand Old Duke of York, neither up nor down, with bells ringing above and below and me deciding which way to go. I think I shall have to issue a list of times when I am available to take calls and then I shall sit and sit and nobody will ring.

If there is anything serious going on in the world that I am unaware of, don't worry. There's nothing I can do about it.

Just put all this down to my delirious condition. I do wish someone would come and chase all these bloody magpies out of my room. I can't think how they got in.

Stop pecking my ear you black and white heathen!

Beware the Ides of March!

See you then,

Your disintegrating P.O.G.

* * *

18 March 1995

All in the wild March-morning I heard the angels call;
It was when the moon was setting, and the dark was over all;
The trees began to whisper, and the wind began to roll,
And in the wild March-morning I heard them call my soul.

Tennyson.

Dear All,

At the beginning of the month I thought that Alfred Lord T was making an accurate prophecy. I was at death's door and expecting 'Fetch' to turn up for my 'Inside Bit' at any moment. ('Fetch', by the way, is a character from a heavenly fantasy telling

188

the adventures of Charles Henry Simkins [deceased] and the Rev Tobias Jug [deceased])

However, Kay Mason assured me that it was her prayers, together with Doctor Moore's antibiotics brought me back into the land of the living. A sudden change in the weather and a few warm sunny days completed the cure. I can now walk as far as the shop if I stay in bottom gear.

Angela did a lot to assist in the cure and arrived to take me to the Anchor Inn for lunch and a medicinal pint of Hardy Country Ale.

Then on the fourteenth day I persuaded Susan and Phillip to join me for a farewell lunch. They were in the throes of packing up and in the hands of the removal people preparing to move to somewhere near Bridport in Dorset. I do not envy them. The mere prospect of moving makes me shudder. However, the lunch and a further libation of ale from Rosemary's capable hands and a mouth-watering lunch from Mrs Howard's kitchen did a lot towards my slow recovery. Three cheers for the Anchor Inn.

Now in the third week of the month I can watch the Cheltenham Festival and be thankful that I am not one of the 55,000 racegoers on the actual course. I can watch the racing from the comfort of my armchair. I am told that the 'On Course' betting averages one million pounds per race and 'Off Course' betting in the region of ninety million pounds over the three days! Bless my soul!

The television programmes do not improve. It seems to be nothing but quiz shows offering fantastic prizes, 'Wish you were here' holiday epics and programmes relating to a new phase of sexuality. One such programme described the doings of two gays adventuring in Amsterdam. I did not watch it. It also seems that there is some dissention on the subject of sexuality among some of our senior clerics. I can't imagine why. I read somewhere that if God had approved of homosexuals it would have been Adam and Steve or Madam and Eve in the Garden of Eden. He even expressed His disapproval by bringing down fire and brimstone on Sodom. I think that they should still be referred to as Sodomites. Look what He did to Lot's wife. Just for looking back over her shoulder as well.

Of course interspersed among all these enticing programmes are the soaps. Australian twice daily and our own collection that seem to thrive around the local pubs. It also seems to me that most of the entertainment is hosted by the female sex. The ladies are taking over everything. Not to worry James. Leave it all to Esther Rantzen and Oprah Winfrey.

At least we have the occasional rugger match. The streets in Alton are paved with gold. I discovered this while on my shopping excursion with Betty. I saw before my eyes a gold one-pound coin on the pavement. I persuaded Betty to pick it up for me together with a one-penny piece also resting beside it. I have allowed Betty to use the pound to purchase a National Lottery ticket for me. Who knows. It may be my lucky day.

This week's *Horse and Hounds* displayed David's advertisement regarding the disposal of Tollard Park Equestrian Centre. I do hope that they will make a successful sale.

What a lot of changes are taking place all at once. I understand that Michael has also moved into Taunton but I have not yet received his 'change of address'.

Our gallant Prime Minister, either to get away from those nasty critics at Westminster or because he has run out of fresh hands to shake in Europe, has descended on the Middle East oozing *bonhomie* and spreading *largesse* on our old friend Mr Marrowfat and the Palestinians. I wonder how Mr Marrowfat manages to keep all that stubble on his face. It never seems to develop into a beard neither does it ever get shaved off – he reminds me of an old fashioned gooseberry with a tea towel on its head. Fancy being kissed on both cheeks by that!

One might have thought that Mr Major had enough problems here at home without the Middle East. Our NHS is in a mess. Our schools are screaming for help. Our transport system is fast becoming the worst in the world and our roads are developing miles of disintegrating surfaces. Anyway I expect King Hussein of Jordan will give him a nice tea before the next Prime Minister's question time. I think that I have bleated on enough. I will now leave you and continue trying to get fit.

My love to you all.

Your struggling P.O.G.

21 March 1995

It was a lover and his lass,
  With a hey, and a ho, and a hey nonino,
That o'er the green cornfield did pass,
  In the springtime, the only pretty ring time,
When birds do sing, hey ding a ding, ding;
  Sweet lovers love the spring.

                                        Shakespeare.

Dear All,

Hooray! Spring is here and the sun is shining. The daffodils are all out and it's sister Hilda's eighty-ninth birthday. I sang Happy Birthday over the phone to her before I got up. She was not happy. Tooth trouble. That's old age for you. Get over one problem and another crops up. Depreciation. Wear and tear of the old system. I wonder what my next malfunction will be?

In the spring a young man's fancy lightly turns to thoughts of Love.

                                        William S again.

The trouble is that I am old. My thoughts only stray round Hardy Country Ale or a rum and dry ginger. No more do I get a stirring up of hormones around my loins when my eyes focus on the charms of a beautiful female. Mind you, beautiful females are few and far between these days. At least within my sphere of activity. I can of course cast my mind back to my youth and my 'snuggle-puffing' days in the porch of Flore Church with my Kathleen. She used to tempt me with the most delicious sandwiches. I was always hungry and she always let me hold her hand afterwards! My mouth waters. That's probably the wrong emotion but it's all I can manage nowadays. Change the subject James.

The golden pavement in Alton did not bring me the Lottery

191

jackpot. In fact only one number out of six. However, I was compensated and Wendy took Betty and me on a mystery tour into the depths of Surrey. Going through Guildford was a feast of nostalgia. We passed St Saviours Church where Hilda was married. I glimpsed the Royal Grammar School where they tried to educate me. Mind you, Guildford now bears little resemblance to the town of my youth. We passed through Merrow and over the Downs to Shere, Albury and Abinger Hammer, Leith Hill and back home below the Hogs Back through Seal where we stopped for a delicious cream tea. Wendy is a splendid driver and kindness itself.

My cup then overflowed as I watched England defeat Scotland and win the Grand Slam. My fingernails will not need cutting for weeks.

But that was not all. A few days later at teatime the doorbell rang and there stood Dereck and Gill Nelson. They had found me at last. What a wonderful surprise. It is so much nicer when friends call unexpectedly.

And now Betty is waiting to take me to do my weekly shopping. Man cannot live on bread alone and I'm nearly out of Lamb's Navy Rum.

Excuse me for a day or so.

Sunday the twenty-sixth. Mother's Day. Wendy invited me out to lunch with Betty. We ventured forth and were soon lost in a welter of traffic. Everyone with a car seemed to be out. The area around Sainsbury's Superstore on the outskirts of Farnham resembled a mobile ant-hill. Arriving at Badshot Lea Garden Centre we found the huge carpark chockablock and every mother and grandmother within a fifty-mile radius being feted by their offsprings. We somehow managed to find a table at which we could eat our Sunday lunch.

The world has completely and irrevocably gone stark raving bonkers. Trollies and baskets were being filled with rose bushes every conceivable bedding plant and garden tool. At least it was an insight on how the present-day family spends their Sundays I thought of the very favoured lady who originated 'Mother's Day' some two thousand years ago and wondered if she felt sad at the dwindling congregations in our churches who still remembered Her. Like Christmas and Easter our religious festivals are prime targets for commercialism.

I find it very sad.

However, Bentley at least is a quiet corner of England. The by-pass is operative. They still have to put the finishing touches to it but I can now walk down to the shop without inhaling carbon monoxide fumes. The Parish Council were filmed drinking Champagne standing in the road with not a motor vehicle in sight. Mind you, the fifty or so houses on this Eggars Field Estate can still produce upwards of eighty cars used for communting and delivering children to school each day.

And now it is Monday. Washing day. British Summer Time has started and I lost an hour's sleep. The sun is still shining and the Weather Forecasters have predicted snow tomorrow. Ah well! Variety is the spice of life. I shall go and erect my washing line and leave you to read and inwardly digest this rubbish.

With love from,

Your bewildered P.O.G.

* * *

7 April 1995

Oh, to be in England
　Now that April's there,
And whoever wakes in England
　Sees, some morning, unaware,
That the lowest boughs and the brushwood sheaf
　Round the elm-tree bole are in tiny leaf,
While the chaffinch sings on the orchard bough
　In England — now!

Robert Browning.
(Home Thoughts from Abroad)

Dear All,

How lucky we are to live here. I am an anglophile. I just love England. I so remember when returning from duty abroad looking down from the plane window and seeing my England looking like a beautiful patchwork of green and gold fields. Home again!

And now all I hear and read are adverts and programmes exhorting me to take a holiday anywhere from Timbuctoo to the North Pole. Everyone talks of holidays and short breaks away from it all.

Madness reigns supreme. I don't even want to wander far from dear old Bentley.

I remember a German officer once saying to me:

'You English won the War and decided that you needed a holiday. You deserved one. The trouble with you is that you have been on holiday ever since.'

I am beginning to think that he was not far wrong.

The P&O Shipping Line have just taken over their new Cruise Flagship. The Queen is to preside over a naming ceremony. The S.S. *Oriana*.

Built in Germany. Hamburg. It gives me food for thought. I think that Her Majesty should suggest that they ask the German Chancellor to do the job.

Poor old England. A few years back we built the best ships in the world.

I am also being pressed to eat any food other than English. I am deluged with suggestions that I take a gastronomic tour of the different regions of India and capture Madhur Jaffrey's 'Flavours of India'. I can get a free forty-eight page sample containing thirty delicious recipes by collecting six tokens from the *Radio Times*. I am urged to discover the world and eat it!

A suggested menu:

Starter:
    Greek Dip Medley or Bang Bang Chicken.
Main Course:
    Hoi Sin Pork or Chicken Tikka Masala.
Dessert:
    Butterscotch or Chocolate Sauce with Nuts.
            All for just £8.99.

Beefburgers. Pastas. Pizzas etc. etc. etc. The list goes on and on

Did I say we are all going mad? I was right!

Did I say Poor old England? I was right!

And Cambridge won the Boat Race. There is no justice.

Stop moaning James! Something good is bound to show up soon.

It did. John descended on me. He was on his way to Heathrow to pick up his wandering wife who was returning from labours in Nice. He was lucky and I was able to produce a prawn salad followed by banana custard. We had a long natter while we ate and got up to date with all John's projects in Dorset.

Then on Thursday my good friends from Reading, Ray and Freda blew in to take me to lunch at the Anchor Inn. There is no shadow of doubt Hardy Country Ale does me a world of good. I love people coming to take me out for lunch. Home economy and entertaining company to boot.

Freda got the giggles. I told her the story of the two bishops discussing pre-marital sex.

1st Bishop: 'I never had sex with my wife before we were married. Did you?'

2nd Bishop: 'No. I don't think so. What was her maiden name?'

It was lovely to see them. And next week Tony and Heather Rudin are coming to enjoy a noggin at the Anchor Inn and I shall be brought up to date on all the additions currently being produced by the younger Rudins.

I know that Jacqueline has just produced a baby son. A perfect specimen. The best in the world. A little godling. It is to be named Maxine after its paternal grandfather.

And now it is Aintree week. The Grand National on Saturday. The Argentine Grand Prix as well. What a feast of entertainment.

Remember also that next week is Holy Week. So reserve a few quiet moments for a little meditation. Say a few prayers and don't forget to mention

P.O.G.

I shall now wish you all a very Happy Easter. My sweet peas are growing. The tomato plants are thriving and the tulips are just bursting into bloom. In fact everything in the garden is lovely.

Sam has now taken up residence on the garden swingseat. Happy Days.

Your once again smiling P.O.G.

EPILOGUE

P.O.G. continues to write his letters as 1995 carries on its daily round.

A check up with Mr Richards, the 'Bellyologist', on 12 June 1995 proved that he was still in the land of the living. To quote Mr Richards after his examination: 'I am very, very pleased with you. I shall not want to see you until this time next year.'

Remember P.O.G.'s motto – K.K.K. at all times – and keep your fingers crossed for him.

God Bless you all.